Finding Peace *in* Life's Storms

Effective Techniques to Cope with Depression

Dr. Monte Miller

Finding Peace in Life's Storms
Copyright © 2022 Dr. Monte Miller

ALL RIGHTS RESERVED. No part of this book publication may be reproduced, stored in a retrieval system, or transmitted in any form or by any means, electronic, mechanical, photocopy, recording, or any other, except brief quotation in reviews, without the prior permission of the author or publisher.

Printed in the United States of America

ISBN 979-8-9872579-1-3

Dedication

This book is dedicated to the hundreds of clients who I have had the honor of trying to bring a little light into the darkened world in which I found them.

It is also dedicated to the Wonderful Counselor, my Savior, and the One person there with me through all of the storms of my life, my Jesus, the only One who deserves all the glory.

Table of Contents

Preface 7
Post-Storm Lessons... 11
Introduction.. 13
Chapter 1 – Don't Let Your Emotions Control You;
You Control Your Emotions..23
Chapter 2 – You Can Choose Your Thoughts 31
Chapter 3 – Happiness Is a Choice 37
Chapter 4 – Are You Grieving? 45
Chapter 5 – Accept What You Cannot Change 53
Chapter 6 – Dangers of Selfishness 61
Chapter 7 – Are Your Expectations Too High?.............73
Chapter 8 – How to Apply Gratitude.............................89
Chapter 9 – Heaven :Our Eternal Home 105
Chapter 10 – How to Make Sense of Suffering 125
Chapter 11 – The Meaning of Life and Our Purpose....135
Chapter 12 – Your Life Is More Than Fair...................147
Chapter 13 – Final Thoughts..155
Monte's Praise Playlist 163
About the Author 165

Preface

"Monte, your father and I have decided to get a divorce."

The first major storm in my life was divorce. My parents divorced when I was eleven years old and my mother, brother, and I had to move into a smaller house. It was very hard for us, especially my mother. I hated spending awkward weekends with my father in his new but tiny apartment. Three months later, my dad decided to move away from our hometown in Dallas to live in Amarillo, so he could marry his childhood sweetheart.

Looking back, I don't remember feeling very stressed, but I had stomach ulcers during that time. So, obviously, I was feeling some measure of stress. Perhaps, I had blocked out the memories of how bad it truly was.

****

"Monte, this is Craig (my step-father). Your mother had a stroke."

When I was fourteen years old, my mother had a stroke. It was a typical stroke. The right side of her body was partially paralyzed. She could not speak properly, and she was much more emotional than she usually was. My mother was quite young, only forty-five at the time. (Little did I know this would foreshadow my future career working with stroke patients.)

My grandparents moved in with us, which was very stressful because my grandfather was one of the grumpiest men who ever lived. Several times, my mother would yell at me for no reason whatsoever due to her emotional dyscontrol. Financially, we were hurting as Mom was unable to work for a long time. Overall, she was a great mother, but life was extremely stressful.

****

"Monte! Come down here, please. Hurry! Something is very wrong!"

Those were some of the last words I heard my mother say on this earth. I was just sixteen. Two years after her first stroke, at just 47, Mom had a second stroke. This one was much more severe. It left her in a coma for one week until she finally passed away. I was in Dallas. My father was still living in Amarillo, and my brother had gone off to Texas A&M. My best friend had also moved away. My older sister and her new husband moved in with me. However, she was grieving and stressed also. I truly appreciate everything she did for me, but all we ever did was fight. This was not just a storm. This was a freaking hurricane!

****

"Monte, I want to break up."

It was my second year at Texas A&M, and my high school/college girlfriend was breaking up with me for another man. Looking back on this now, it seems like such a minor storm. I had already wanted to break up with her, but the fact that she broke up with me was an insult to my ego! At the time, it was devastating. I felt unlovable. I fell into a serious depression, and it took me several months to pull out of it.

****

"_____"

No "Monte" quote this time. Just cold silence. My wife of 20 years rolled over once again and went to sleep. She wasn't angry or upset, just off in her own world, forgetting about me again. I had given her my whole heart for years, but no matter what I tried, not much affection was returned. I spent many hours in my car before and after work, depressed, wondering what more I could do to get her to love me back. This was not a big storm as much as it was a very long, cold, rainy night.

****

"Monte, you're not going to get paid for all those sessions you were billing for all these months. You've paid out tens of thousands of dollars but will not be reimbursed for most of it."

A bad divorce agreement (thanks to my stupid lawyer), Obamacare, and the resulting changes to the insurance companies and payouts, my billing company failing to keep up with the changes, and several high medical expenses with the family left me high and dry financially. I sold my beloved house to make ends meet, only to have all the equity eaten up by insurance problems.

We have all had storms that created stress and left us unable to pay our bills. But I didn't expect it to happen to me. Why should it? I had my doctorate degree and my own successful practice for 20 years, which by most accounts was still thriving clinically, just not economically.

****

Post-Storm Lessons

Life Can Be Hard and Depressing

When you were young, your future seemed bright and full of hope. You had expectations and dreams. And then reality set in. Whether through your own mistakes or those of others, things did not go your way, and life started to sink. You get discouraged, overwhelmed, helpless, and hopeless.

Life hits us hard like fierce storms, which I refer to as the *storms of life*. We can all be overwhelmed by these storms. We all get depressed at some time, especially when we have had to weather many storms. Sometimes it seems as if life, in general, is just one big storm.

What do you do when the storms of life arise? Can you find peace in their midst?

I did not share the stories of storms in my life to play the victim and cry poor me. I am nothing special. Some of my experiences were traumatic and affected me for a long time. However, many people have had storms much worse than mine. Plus, I must admit I contributed to my storms, and sadly, to the storms in other people's lives.

Despite my sorrows, I have also had my share of blessings, which I will talk about in this book. A big part of getting

Introduction

through storms is appreciating the good in our lives. Overall, I have been a positive, happy person. But the truth is storms are real and can be devastating for all of us. We may not be able to choose if we experience storms or not, but we can choose how we deal with them.

My storms are nothing compared to those of some of my clients at the nursing homes, which I will share with you later. You cannot end up in a nursing home without going through terrible storms. Then you are hit with them every day thereafter, without any hope they will end, at least, not in this life. I have spent the last twenty years compassionately listening to those who have been through hell and back. Many of these people have learned to find deep peace and contentment despite their storms. You can too.

In this book, I don't only share stories about life's storms but effective techniques to find peace in the storm and conquer depression in this chaotic world. The pain and trauma from life's storms are real. And it will never be an easy journey. But peace can be found.

"And the peace of God which transcends all understanding will guide your hearts and your minds in Christ Jesus" (Philippians 4:7 NIV).

Introduction

"From the ends of the earth, I cry to you for help when my heart is overwhelmed." (Psalm 61:2)

Helping Others through Storms

My role in life for the past twenty-five years has been to hold umbrellas for people during terrible storms. I have learned the lessons in this book through my work with people of all ages, but especially through my work with the wonderful old folks in my nursing homes. These lessons are not just applicable to older people or those in bad health situations. I have applied them to this book to help many others. We can all learn a great deal from the struggles of the elderly.

Many times, I feel sorry for myself due to the storms I am going through. But when I go to work and see how some of these guys handle much more severe storms than mine, it motivates me. It makes me feel downright foolish to be so depressed about my relatively small problems.

I will share a little bit about my work and the nature of my clients' problems. I want you to know that I do not just know about storms from my own life, but from experiencing others' severe problems as well. We can learn from those who have lost everything and learned to cope. Young, healthy people have no idea how incredibly difficult it is to deal with all the challenges that come with severe health issues and getting older. Most of the storms for these folks are extreme and will last the rest of their lives. Sometimes the storms last for just a few months, but other times, they last for twenty years or more. Some people handle these crises amazingly well, considering their situations. But, of course, many do not.

Many of the ones who are doing well now did not do well at first. They struggled with depression and despair but pulled themselves out. They did this, not because they were inherently stronger or smarter, though they did have the wisdom to learn how to change their perspective on their problems. Some improved on their own, and I just learned from them.

Let me give you a taste of the storms in my patients' lives. Many of them suffer from diabetes. This chronic disease can ravage the body, causing blindness, kidney failure, and leg amputations. Some have been stricken with cancer, Parkinson's disease, and other debilitating illnesses that leave their minds intact but render their bodies useless. All of them have endured extreme losses: their houses, pets, beloved spouses, and others. They cannot drive anymore, play golf, or go to their social clubs. But I have also dealt with forty and fifty-year-olds who had severe strokes and found themselves completely dependent upon others. What is worse is that they will have to live at a facility for the next thirty years or so of their lives! One day they will be normal, the next day totally dependent. These are but some of the medical issues that can ruin lives.

Indeed, living with medical Illnesses is serious. However, there are also the challenges of everyday life in a nursing home. Most of the homes I worked at were good homes. But life is tough when you have to wait for someone to meet your every need. Imagine what it is like having to wait for caregivers to take you to the bathroom every time. And if they are too busy with others, then you just have to wet yourself. Getting used to living in a small room with a stranger when you are used to having a four-bedroom house with a lifetime of furniture, pictures, knick-knacks, and memories, is extremely difficult and depressing.

However, the most difficult loss that every single one of my clients had to deal with is the loss of independence, freedom, and control. Psychologically, this is the worst part of their suffering. It is emotional torture. Pain and loss of loved ones are terrible, but the inability to make simple, everyday decisions when most of your options are taken away and you have to be told what to do all the time, is demoralizing. Many have even lost the freedom to get across the room to get their hairbrush.

These amazing people were just like you and me. And then life's storms arose and changed everything. They had every reason to be depressed and anxious. But many of them learned how to find as much peace as possible. They found ways to beat the depression these storms brought on.

Practice What You Preach
In the middle of writing this book, I was in the center of several other big storms myself. I was already struggling with

the leftover problems from past storms when *boom*, another big storm hit. For the past ten years, as of the final editing of this book, there was one big storm after another. It is true that in life, you are either in a storm, coming out of a storm, or heading into a storm.

I finally came out of all those issues and life started to improve. But I always leaned on the principles of this book to get me through, never caving into depression very deeply or for long despite feeling extremely overwhelmed at times.

I dearly believe in the truths behind this book. I have witnessed all types of people put these perspectives in place with great changes in their ability to cope and a huge improvement in the quality of their lives. Hence, I cling to these principles.

A good thing about my job is that I am always encouraging someone else, which then causes me to think of these same concepts and apply them to my life. A primary component of good psychotherapy is genuineness. I hate insincerity. What good am I as a therapist if I do not believe in what I am selling to my clients?

I know speakers are more credible when they have gone through similar situations to what they are discussing. I believed in the techniques and principles in this book long before I wrote them out. But putting them into practice after writing them down has convinced me even more.

Depression and Storms

Depression and storms often go hand in hand. So when storms enter our lives, depression and anxiety often follow. Therefore, in this book, we look primarily at how to handle the strong, overwhelming emotions that overshadow us as a result of storms. Certainly, many people have long-standing depression with or without storms, and they can also benefit from these concepts. However, the main purpose of this book is to help those who suffer from depression because of the storms of life. In some cases, long-standing depression can start after a storm, and become very difficult to get rid of.

Major Depressive Disorder is a unique medical condition because it can be part medical and part psychological. It can fall anywhere on the spectrum from one end to the other. Some people are born with a natural tendency toward depression, or it can be learned. Others have physiological depression in their family history. Depression is there regardless of the level of stress in their environments. However, other people are psychologically depressed simply because they have experienced trauma such as the loss of a loved one.

I do not want to minimize the suffering of those who are severely medically depressed. Medical intervention from a psychiatrist is needed for these people. However, do not throw out any of the techniques in this book just because you have medical-based depression. Your physical brain may have initially caused the depression, but the way the mind thinks can be altered in a harmful manner. Thus, retraining your mind is necessary. In addition, storms will still cause negative irrational thinking that must be fought with more positive rational thinking, regardless of your medical disposition.

Depression can hit us out of nowhere. We don't choose to be depressed. We just are. Biological depression can occur suddenly for no real psychological reason. However, sudden depressed feelings can also hit us without any physiological basis. It can be difficult to tell the difference.

Even though it seems that these feelings appeared from out of nowhere, thoughts are actually triggering them. But we seldom realize it. Stressful events are inevitable, and they are accompanied by distressing thoughts. Depression is then a natural result of these thoughts. The problem is that we do not always remember having depressing thoughts. However, we are still stuck with the left-over emotions the thoughts caused. A big part of therapy and learning to cope with the storm is becoming more self-aware of the thoughts and assumptions going on in your head.

Stroke with One Hand. Punch with the Other
The very first lesson on the first day of my very first psychotherapy class in my master's degree program has stuck with me to this day. Professor Fran White at Wheaton College taught us a profound principle. I thank her for this and many other lessons. I am not sure if she came up with this on her own or not but she said, "Good therapy is stroking with one hand, while punching with the other."

Both of these components are essential to help clients get to a better place and cope with their storms. Therapists must be empathetic and show compassion, yet, push their patients to view their lives differently, even if it is uncomfortable in the beginning. Of course, the therapist must first comfort them and then confront them. Unfortunately, many therapists stop at the point where they only provide comfort. But that will only help the client feel better for a short time. It will not generate growth.

I take my client's storms very seriously. I pride myself on taking as much time as necessary during typical counseling sessions to give support and understanding. In some cases, I have had to spend a year gaining the trust of certain clients. I know I cannot just jump right into giving advice without first getting to know the person's emotional pain. People who are suffering need to feel heard and have their feelings validated.

In this book, I will give many alternative views on facing problems. The focus will be on the solutions. Due to the very nature of this format, I must make assumptions and cannot take all background information and situations into account. Please forgive me if some proposed solutions seem contrite or simplistic. A simple answer may be all the help you need, not because you are simple, but because it causes you to see your situation differently.

Any self-help psychology book, blog, or YouTube video, is by nature, generalized advice. Such advice cannot be taken as psychotherapy. It cannot be taken as full knowledge of your specific situation and handled with the compassion and sensitivity that your issues deserve as if you were in counseling. However, fair warning, I will punch. I will make many suggestions that point the finger back at you. This does not necessarily mean you caused your storm, but you may not have been dealing with it the best way. Thus, it could be making your storm worse. We all need to be punched sometimes. Growth can be quite painful. If the answers were easy or obvious, you would not need this book.

All I ask is to just give these ideas a chance. To use these ideas, you must take a serious step back; be humble and honest with yourself, and question if you can look at your situation in a better way. Maybe it means letting go of the things you wanted or accepting something you did not want to accept. But do not dismiss *any* idea at first glance. You owe it to your future happiness to consider all options. The pain and trauma from life's storms are real. And it will never be an easy journey. But peace can be found. "And the peace of God which transcends all understanding will guide your hearts and your minds in Christ Jesus" (Philippians 4:7 NIV).

As you read each chapter, you will not only discover stories about life's storms but effective, tried, and true techniques of Cognitive Behavioral Therapy to help you find peace in the storm and conquer depression in this chaotic world. I will use these techniques to teach you how to become more aware of the thoughts in your head so you can learn to control your emotions, instead of letting your emotions control you. I will teach you happiness is ultimately your choice, even when terrible storms and life situations have hit you and you have been victimized and traumatized.

I will teach you new ways of looking at your situation. When we are in a storm, we get stuck only being able to see the same limited view of ourselves and have limited ideas of how to get out of the storm. With the perspective of opening up yourself to new ideas firmly in place, I will help you use new analogies (parables) to find new solutions.

Some of these new views include comparing your struggles to grieving. This is especially important if your storm is the loss of a loved one, but it is also helpful for us all, in any storm. We will look at the concept of acceptance and how basic stubbornness, pride, and selfishness can prevent happiness. Let me explain these concepts, and take an honest look at yourself. You will reap great rewards.

Sometimes it can be difficult to see God's love and control in the midst of a storm. We question why a good loving God allows us to suffer. I will firmly address this difficult question, primarily because it has a direct impact on how we cope with our storms.

Join me on this journey of growth and strength. Expand your view of your life and defeat depression. It may not be easy. You might have to accept things you do not want to accept. It will take courage. But you can do this. You must do this to change your life. And in doing so, you will find Peace in Your Storm.

Chapter 1

Don't Let Your Emotions Control You; You Control Your Emotions

"As a man thinks, so is he" (Proverbs 23:7).

Cognitive Behavioral Therapy: Thoughts – Feelings – Behaviors

To change our perspective on our storms, we must first understand how our minds work. So we will explore Cognitive Behavioral Therapy (CBT), which I use primarily in psychotherapy. It is one of the oldest and arguably the most studied and effective ways of looking at our lives and our problems and finding the best methods to cope with life in the best way possible. I will briefly describe it to you to help you understand your emotions and how to learn to control them.

Think of a triangle with three points. Your thoughts or beliefs are at one end, your emotions at another, and your behaviors on the other. Each of these points can cause changes in the other two. Everything we talk about in this book is one of these three points. Knowing how each one affects the other two can help you gain more control over your situation. In any given situation, we have dozens of different thoughts that come into our minds, many of which we are not even aware exist. Yet, they affect us strongly. Several of these thoughts will contradict each other. Also, I do not care how smart you are, some thoughts will be irrational, silly, petty, childish, or sinful. Some thoughts may be perfectly rational, given a tough situation, but it is not helpful to continue dwelling on those thoughts.

These thoughts are learned from a variety of sources. Our parents and lessons learned in childhood shape our thoughts, assumptions, and expectations. Our thoughts are also shaped by our early school environments, social and sexual experiences, our first romantic relationships, breakups, and heartaches. Mass and social media heavily influence these thoughts.

The evaluations we make about our self-esteem, need for love, fear of abandonment, sense of accomplishment, and purpose in life must all be understood. Our mental toughness and ability to handle stress, moral reasoning, self-centeredness, and compassion, are key thoughts that shape our mental health.

We learn to think about life, others, and ourselves through all of the above types of thoughts. Problems come up, I believe, because of faulty logic in our thoughts. Everything makes sense to us at the moment. However, when we take a step back and become more self-aware of these little thoughts, we can re-examine them in a healthier light, see the better logic, and get rid of the problematic thoughts that bring us down.

Do Not Trust the "Truth" of Your Emotions

Specifically, you need to know that your mind works in coordination with your emotions. Unfortunately, this is not always a good thing because our emotions can change with the wind. However, the truth of our situation does not change. The truth is not usually all good or all bad but a combination of both. However, the truth is what it is. It does not change based on your view of it. This is the same for the truth of God, just as it is for the truth of your situation. God is who He is. We may have our own opinions of Him, but He is who He is, regardless of our perspectives.

What is the truth of your situation? That is a complicated question. There are many ways of looking at it. Obviously, your situation is bad, or you would not be here reading this. A storm is obviously a storm. What is God's perspective on your situation? After all, God's perspective is the truth. Therefore, in this book, I will try to give you many different perspectives on what God's view might be of your situation. If you can see your situation more accurately from God's perspective, you will be much better equipped to change your attitude about it and gain the strength to cope.

Warning: Emotions Lie!
You cannot trust your thoughts when emotional. They will lie to you. You will think your view is the truth, that it is real and valid. Sometimes, it may very well be true, but you cannot rely on it. This is a very important, fundamental point. When we are in a storm or recovering from a storm, we are naturally going to be very emotional. When we are emotional, our thinking can become illogical and unreliable. But the problem is not just the errors in thinking; it is also that we think we have better insight into our lives during these emotional times than we normally do and then react impulsively to these new insights. Emotions can be wonderful, but

they can lead us astray when making big decisions in our lives, especially during life's storms.

During these times, your thoughts might get very dramatic and lead you astray from a true and accurate assessment of the situation. If you assess the situation wrong, you are more likely to act in a way that will get you into trouble and make your problem worse. You can act on the different base emotions. You can be depressed and give up. You can be angry and lash out verbally, or be physically violent. If you are anxious, you can have a panic attack, or be stressed out; this hurts your health. Having said that, it is also possible to be overly positive and react in too grandiose a manner. Consequently, you may overly commit to doing something foolhardy.

I Love You...I Hate You
To demonstrate my point, I want to give an example of a former relative in my life who is an extremely emotional person. This is an extreme case, but it illustrates how you can change your thinking based on the emotions you feel at the time.

Overall, in my opinion, this relative has a fair marriage. However, when she is unhappy with her husband, he is a "no good son of a ------." At that moment, she feels she hates him and she tells him in front of her children that she thinks he is no good, wishes she had never married him, and the marriage was the worst mistake of her life. However, when she is happy, she says he is the best thing that ever happened to her and they are so deeply in love.

If you ask her when she's happy about the negative thoughts, she will say, "I was just being silly when angry. You know how I get. That's not the truth. The truth is that he's a good man, and I'm happily married." However, when she is angry and is asked, she will tell you, "The truth is he really is no good, and I'm just fooling myself when I try to pretend he is a good husband."

There is no in-between with her. It is either one side or the other. Her view of truth is swayed by whatever she happens to feel at the moment. Truth does not work like that. Truth is truth, and it does not change depending on how we feel, our emotions, or anything else. In this woman's case, the truth is that her husband is a decent but not perfect guy, and they have a decent marriage, except for the fact that she overreacts too often.

There Might Be Truth, But Do Not Overreact

I hope this example illustrates how all of us can think and act when emotional, especially during storms. I hope your view of your life does not vary this dramatically in normal life. However, when terrible things happen to us, any of us can let our emotions overtake our logical thoughts and turn everything upside down—and often in a dramatic way.

Now, it is possible your thinking is correct when you are upset. Just because you are emotional does not mean you are wrong. However, you cannot trust your thoughts at that moment. If you calm down and over a period of time and through different emotions, you are still thinking the same things, then you might be seeing things accurately. You should act accordingly.

Additionally, because your situation is truly bad, your emotional mind might make it much worse than it would be otherwise. For example, when you think your husband is being a jerk, he might really be treating you meanly. However, this does not mean he is terrible and worth yelling at or divorcing. You may think you should divorce him at the moment, but that is faulty thinking and harmful to you if you overreact, although he was mean.

In a different example, perhaps you have messed up, failed, and caused problems. That may be true, but it does not mean you are a failure and your situation is hopeless. That is not the truth, even if you have failed at something.

Life is never fully hopeless. Have you made mistakes? We all have. Are you hopeless and helpless? Probably not. Are you unlovable? No, absolutely not. Have you done things that are not fully lovable? Maybe. Maybe you have been perfectly fine and other people around you have not appreciated you; they have hurt you. You have every right to be hurt, but it does not mean people will always hurt you.

Are you feeling empty because of the loss you had in your life? Yes, probably. Will you feel empty for the rest of your life? No. These questions are what your emotional, scared mind is trying to answer. But the truth is never as dramatic as your fears are leading you to believe. Do not trust the irrational fears. They will not help you. They can only harm you.

Chapter Takeaways

1. Thoughts lead to emotions. Identify all the thoughts, especially the little irrational ones.
2. The more emotional you are, the less you should trust your thoughts. Thus, do not trust your emotions.

Chapter 2

You Can Choose Your Thoughts

"We take captive every thought to make it obedient to Christ" (2 Corinthians 10:5).

I want this book to bring you hope that you can overcome the problems and storms of this world. You can learn to control your emotions. You can learn to view your world, your problems, and even your relationship with Christ in a new way. Changing your viewpoint, your focus, and your attitude, can make all the difference in the world. Unfortunately, this does not always change or get rid of the storm, but it will change your ability to stand up to it. Hope comes in the power to choose. We can purposely control our thoughts. This is not easy to do at all. But if we can control our thoughts, we can regain a little more control in our lives.

Firetrucks

Do an experiment with me, please. Think of a big, red firetruck, with all the details. Picture it in your mind. Imagine the firemen in their suits and hats, the ladders, hoses, and the Dalmatian riding on the truck. Now stop. Stop thinking of the red fire truck. Do not think of the red fire truck. No truck. No ladder. No Dalmatian. Stop. No firetruck. No firetruck.

Not thinking of the red fire truck is difficult when I keep talking about a red fire truck, right? Okay, now think about a yellow taxicab. An old sedan, painted yellow, with a band of black and white checkerboard pattern around it. It has a little white sign on the top that says, "Taxi." Do you have it pictured in your mind now? Guess what? You stopped thinking of the firetruck. This is a simple demonstration to show you can choose what you think, but only with certain strategies. You cannot stop thinking about your storm if that is all you are focused on. However, if you replace it with a completely different thought, the first thought goes away.

There are many different strategies that this book will explain to help you control your thoughts better. For now, just keep an open mind to the power God has given you to be a free thinker. The Bible is full of examples and encouragement to think about more godly things. God made us. He knows we think and what we choose to think about will lead us to either a joyful and holy place, or a darker and more depressing place.

"Some people complain about the thorns on their rosebush. Other people are just happy that there's roses on their thornbush."—Abraham Lincoln

Team Roses or Team Thorns?
Ah, yes—the wisdom I have learned from the walls of the local Cracker Barrel restaurant! I later learned that the earlier quote was attributed to Abraham Lincoln. This is such a great saying because it describes our lives and our choices,

and illustrates our attitudes toward our lives. It is a beautiful illustration.

In everybody's life, there are roses and thorns. You cannot get away from either. Sometimes the thorns greatly outnumber the roses. It may be an undeniable fact that there are storms (thorns) in your life. But it is also *always* true that there are good things (roses).

How do you see life then? You have a choice; you know. Do you believe life is supposed to be full of roses and how dare there be thorns? Or do you believe life will necessarily have thorns but thank goodness there are some roses? These are two distinctly different attitudes toward life. Which viewpoint will you embrace?

Take the old saying, "Is the glass half empty or is it half-full?" Both statements are true. Half of the liquid remains and a half has been consumed. You can choose what you want to emphasize. Similarly, life has thorns. Life has roses. What are you going to focus on?

Indeed, the thorns are real and this fact does not need to be validated. However, it does not change the reality that the other side of the equation is true. There are always roses. We will get more into the topic of appreciation later. For now, recognize you have the choice to focus on the good in your life. There are probably many more roses in your life than you notice, even if your situation is not good. As you continue reading, this book will help open your eyes to the roses and assist you in focusing your attention on them. These roses are especially big and beautiful when you look at them from a Christian perspective.

Another popular expression I could have used is when life gives you lemons, make lemonade. A million different funny offsets of this phrase have been given, "When life gives lemons, make margaritas." The choice you have in life is still in the story you make out of what you are given. You have the choice to pucker up and cry over the lemons or try to make something useful out of what life has given you.

Evaluating All the Evidence

Think of how you view your life. Imagine it like a courtroom and you are the judge. Your job is to evaluate yourself, your life, and different concepts of how to see your storms. Truly, this is what you have already been doing, whether you know it or not. You have been examining evidence and coming up with verdicts on big and small issues.

At any given moment, there are pieces of evidence in your life that indicate there is good; there is happiness in your life, and you are a decent person. Of course, there are also pieces of evidence that indicate your life is in bad shape. There could be good evidence that you are a bad person, or, at least, you have failed at times. Our thoughts act as a judge, trying to figure out what the facts are, and what we think about our reality.

We do not just judge if the situation is good or bad, but we also judge the severity of the crime and the punishment that goes along with it. Unfortunately, we are very poor judges.

We let a small amount of evidence sway us in a certain direction. When a storm hits our lives and we are depressed, we tend to emphasize the evidence that life is bad and ignore all the evidence that contradicts this theory. We choose not to consider that there is hope.

We also tend to over-interpret the severity of the crime and the punishment. As I previously explained, we typically make the crime seem much worse than it really was. Did your spouse hurt you? Maybe he did. But, as a judge, when you are angry, can you weigh the evidence of all the good your spouse has done for you, not just the bad? In addition, do not punish others or yourself too harshly when you are guilty of a crime.

Remember God's grace and mercy when evaluating the severity of the punishment you will inflict on someone who hurt you, especially when you are the one guilty of hurting yourself. You do not want to be too lenient and let people run all over you. But you do not want to be too harsh either. Let rationality and God's example be your guide when assessing your reactions to hurts and storms, not emotions.

Chapter Takeaways

1. You are not helpless in your suffering. You *can change* your thoughts; you can change your emotions, and thus, you can change your coping.
2. At least try to consider looking at your situation differently by changing your thoughts

3. Try to look at the more positive perspective, especially when it is God's truth.
4. Consider all the evidence, not just what supports your sadness.

Chapter 3

Happiness Is a Choice

"We take captive every thought to make it obedient to Christ" (2 Corinthians 10:5).

The last chapter was intended to introduce personal choice into your coping. Let us continue that thought by looking at your responsibility in your own life, regardless of if you have been victimized by life. You have choices. You can choose how you see your life, your storms, and your place with God. Again, you may not be able to choose or control the storms that hit you. However, you *can* choose how you cope with them. Actually, you *must* choose how you cope. But It may not be a good choice, one you are not even aware you are making.

You may not feel you have any choice when you are being tossed and turned helplessly by the waves. However, choosing to do nothing is a choice. You choose to do nothing and get overwhelmed and depressed, or you choose to fight it. But you must choose. Think of it like being on a railroad track. If you just sit there and do nothing, you have made your choice, and it will not end well when the train comes.

Since you have choices, it also means that you have personal responsibility. You are accountable for what you are in control of—your responses to the storms. Personal responsibility means you cannot just sit still and cry victim forever. It is normal to get depressed during tough times, but do not give in to it.

You can choose to keep fighting or give in to the sadness. If you give in, you are the one making your life more miserable than it already is. Despite whoever or whatever originally caused the storm, *you* are now contributing to the problem. I know you do not want to be a part of the problem. I know that because you have chosen to read this book. Choose to read more. Choose to question yourself more. And choose to grow.

Happiness Is a Choice
In today's social media world, lots of self-diagnosing occurs, and all kinds of made-up "disorders" exist. Everything is a new trauma. I am not dismissing the fact that people are experiencing real mental health issues, nor am I minimizing anyone's true trauma. However, a growing culture of victimization is out there. Many are helpless victims now. It is not your fault that you happened to be born with "Rejection Sensitivity Disorder" (not a real disorder according to the DSM. We all are sensitive to rejection). People use the word "disorder" to imply that life has hit them with something and everyone must be sensitive to their plight and not hold them accountable for their inability to cope.

I love the title of the book, *Happiness Is a Choice*, by Minirth and Meier. It is a great book that describes basic Cognitive Behavioral Therapy. But the title says it all. We are not helpless victims of life. We can all choose to make the best of our lives and learn to be content. My experience with those going through severe traumas and losses proves that even when you have lost everything with no hope of things getting better, you can still choose to make the most of it. Alternatively, you can choose to be more miserable than your situation has already made you.

Why We Secretly Like Being in the Storm
Do you want to be depressed? I know. That sounds like a ridiculous question. Why would anyone ever want to be depressed? On one hand, of course, you do not want to be depressed. Who would? Nobody truly enjoys being depressed. However, there are subtle reasons why many people choose to be depressed without even knowing they are doing so. Please consider these points; do not dismiss them yet.

On a basic, purely logical level, people would only want to be depressed if they think it would be to their advantage. Be aware that when I say someone would "want" to be depressed, I do not mean on a conscious level. We automatically learn through natural consequences—through rewards and punishments. If we do something and there is some pleasurable event, we learn to repeat that behavior. Conversely, if we have negative consequences from our behavior, we learn not to repeat it.

Take a typical child, for example. He is stressed and depressed about a presentation at school. He then becomes ill, mostly due to stress. His parents let him stay home from school. He gets out of an assignment that he was dreading. His brain just formed a connection without even realizing it.

The connection is between being depressed and getting out of stress. In the academic world, we call this "secondary gains," that is, the benefits one gets unintentionally from one's behavior.

Sometimes, you are not trying to avoid something by being depressed. Maybe you are trying to accomplish something. You want others to know how much you are hurting. Then maybe they would change and treat you better. There are several other possible ways that depression can be used to manipulate a relationship, some obvious, and some completely unconscious. These relationship styles are too complex to get into detail here but can include things like playing the victim as a lifelong personality and wanting people to feel sorry for you.

There are many reasons why someone might get something out of being depressed. Just consider you might be getting more than you realize out of it. I don't want this to sound accusatorial. So let me look at the log that was in my eye first. My personal issue might help shed some light on how these thoughts can easily creep in. At one point, I had to consider that I was guilty myself, and I indeed was. But realizing this and admitting it to myself helped me to deal with my life much better.

My Secret Desire to be Depressed

In the past, I was not just depressed about my situation, but I also realized there was a part of me that wanted to be depressed. In my first marriage, I was depressed for many years. I could not figure out how to get my wife to return my affection and start loving me back. I knew all the books. I knew all the strategies. I have been studying how to be a good husband since I was 15 (not that I'm at all perfect at it!). But no matter what I did, she still took me for granted and did not return my affection.

I would lay in my car in between driving from the different nursing homes and just take long depressed naps. I felt helpless. Over and over again I asked myself, "What can I do to make this work?" I was feeling down more and more, and that went against how I usually approached my life.

Being the good little shrink, I started analyzing myself and my depression, which was serving a purpose, at least, an attempted purpose. I had to admit to myself that I wanted to be depressed. I figured out that I was trying to get my wife to see how depressed I was. I hoped she would then try harder to be a better wife and meet me halfway so I would be happier.

But in analyzing myself I had to accept the reality this was not going to work. She was not going to notice or care enough. Our marriage would not be a happy one. Now, I was just more depressed than I ever was before. I had to swallow my pride, admit defeat, bite the bullet, and accept I cannot change her, and that I am not going to get what I want from her.

But I did not need to let her bring me down further in the process. I still needed to enjoy my life as much as possible, even more so if she was not going to fulfill me. Getting depressed was not going to solve my marriage problems. I could not control her through my depression. This was still not an easy period for me, and I was never able to reach the level of happiness I desired until I divorced and remarried. But that is another story.

Many other options can work to save a marriage, but depression is not one of them. It may be an all too common result of a bad marriage, but it is not a good strategy, conscious or unconscious.

Our Search for Our Fairy Godmother

In my example, I wanted to be depressed to get my wife to notice me. However, the motive for wanting to be depressed is not always to get attention. Sometimes, you just want someone, anyone, to help.

I know this will sound silly, irrational even, but this is how humans work. We all have irrational thoughts and growth comes by admitting, acknowledging, and changing these thoughts. Deep inside our minds, there is a part of us that might think these things can happen magically. We feel if we cry enough and if we are sad enough, our fairy godmother will hear us and come fix all of our problems. Or maybe our knight in shining armor will come and rescue us. Silly, right? Logically, we know this will not happen, but since when are our hearts logical? Look at yourself and your situation, and do not be afraid to admit you have some secret but unrealistic fantasies about someone rescuing you.

This is understandable given how we first learn about the world. Think about the very first thing we learn as humans.

When we are hungry or uncomfortable and wearing a dirty diaper, what happens? We cry. And then? Our needs are magically met by our parents! Thus, we can see how we developed this belief that a magical being will help us, and all we have to do is cry. You are not a baby though. You are much more realistic and logical. You know there is no magic savior in a mother, be it a fairy godmother or natural. But you still have a little boy or girl in you with magical hopes. Tell the damsel in distress in you that she will have to save herself.

Unfortunately, even if being depressed results in some secondary gain, is it worth the cost? Depression is not fun. You are ultimately making yourself sad to be happy. No, you are making yourself unhappy in an ***attempt*** to make yourself happy. This strategy almost always results in years of sadness with no real, long-term, positive results.

Chapter Takeaways

1. You are not a helpless victim of depression, despite being an innocent victim of someone else causing your storm.
2. You can choose to handle your storm more positively, thus, being more content or happy
3. Understand and then fight your thoughts that push you to want to be depressed
4. Give up on the idea that depression will lead to magical solutions

Chapter 4

Are You Grieving?

"Blessed are they that mourn: For they shall be comforted" (Matthew 5:4).

Grieving: Not Just for the Death of Loved Ones

Sometimes, the storms of life bring about a degree of loss, and, at other times, it brings excessive loss. The death of a loved one is a tragic storm that can be very overwhelming. However, it's not just the loss of a loved one that causes us to grieve. Anytime you lose something important, it counts as grieving. A loss is a loss, and we will automatically become sad and grieve. No one looks down on someone who is grieving the loss of a loved one.

We all accept that it is normal to be terribly sad when someone close to us dies. It is known that the survivor will hurt and need time to recover. There is no judging there. In the same manner, people should understand that it is normal to be sad and grieve any other significant losses. You will soon see that both tangible and intangible losses can be more than you may have first realized. But you must give yourself a break and grieve all of your losses.

Realizing All Types of Losses

There are many types of losses, and, in most storms, we lose something important. What have you lost as a result of your storm? It is an important question to ask yourself. You must figure out all the different things you have lost. These can be tangible or intangible. Tangible losses include the loss of a loved one, either through death or the ending of the relationship, but can also include the loss of a pet or a friend. Losing a job, home, hobby, or career, is also a significant tangible loss.

Significant health problems, illness, or injury, especially when permanent can bring about major life changes and losses. Freedom of movement is lost, and usually, huge financial losses are involved. However, the intangible losses during storms are even more devastating psychologically. They are often naturally paired with the above losses but are harder to identify. For example, when you experience a breakup with a loved one, you also lose the future you had hoped for. You lose the love, the good times, the sense of security, and the sense of belonging.

After working for several years, I learned something that my schooling did not teach. My clients are those dealing with serious health problems in nursing homes. Of course, I knew there would be sad because of health problems and the losses of their spouses, homes, and pets. But they taught me that the most traumatic loss every single one of them had to encounter is the loss of independence, personal freedom, and control.

Other intangible losses for many people in all kinds of situations are the loss of innocence, the loss of childhood, and the loss of a sense of purpose. These can include the loss of any idealized dream —the ideal future that you hoped and thought you would have. The real loss is that which your heart is aching for.

Many times, one storm includes multiple losses, both tangible and intangible. As an example, a divorce not only brings about the loss of the person you once loved, but it also causes you to lose time with your children (or even the complete loss of the relationship with your child if the other parent puts the child in the middle of the conflict, as with my storm). It can also cause financial loss, as well as the loss of a house and half of your material possessions.

When a marriage ends in divorce it has its distinct losses. When we marry, we hope and expect our dreams have been answered by the security of having someone with us. That is now gone. Our egos can be devastated by the rejection we experience. If you have a spouse who does not love you or show any affection to you and it is your idea to divorce, it is heartbreaking. You must come to grips with the fact the person does not love you and will never be capable of doing so. That was the reason to divorce in the first place, right? Losing your pride can also be a big loss. You hate admitting to others that you failed at such a big issue in life. Divorce is a major storm that can have multiple losses on multiple levels. However, as with all storms, you can get through the grieving process more quickly if you can identify all the different losses.

Even good events in your life can bring about necessary losses. The birth of the desired child or a new marriage can cause you to lose your freedom, and, in the case of children, sleep. Long-awaited retirement can take away your sense of purpose. These positive changes in your life may be stressful and overwhelming. You may wonder why a positive event leaves you feeling sad. You miss the comfortable routine and familiar life you lost. Realizing this does not make you change your mind about the joy of your new life, but it can help you to better adapt to the changes.

Death

There are many good books on how to survive grieving the death of a loved one. This book will briefly look exclusively at surviving the death of a loved one; however, most of the points made here can be extremely helpful in coping with death, in general, as well as any other loss. This book will not reexamine the stages of grief, though that information is very helpful. I encourage you to read and learn more about this topic.

Let us look briefly at grieving the death of someone we love, and then we will apply these strategies to other types of storms and losses. The sudden death of a loved one creates shock. Our brains have a hard time processing information. It is too much to comprehend. Logically, we know the person is dead, but our hearts cannot accept it. We search desperately for some other answer, some other possibility. We try to bargain with God. Surely, if I agree to be good, then He would perform a miracle and bring the person back. We think maybe the death was a joke, a cruel trick. Maybe the doctors could still do something. We just shout in the middle of the night, No! No! No! No! He can't be gone!" It takes us months or years for our hearts to fully accept the reality that our loved one is not coming back.

In addition to the obvious losses, many other losses go along with death. We don't only lose the tangible loved one; we also lose the intangibles of the relationship: our hopes, dreams, and ambitions for our future with that person. We lose the love we thought would have been ours for life. We must realize these intangible losses and grieve them as well.

Hope Is Not Always a Good Thing

Hope. It is a great word. It fills us with a positive view of the future. We can get through storms because we *hope* things will get better. Hope can give us the strength we need to go on one more day. The foundation of hope is positive *expectations* that things will get better. This is a good thing. We need *this* hope. Hope, that very well can come true, is good.

However, for the sake of helping the grief process, we must examine a different side of hope—the dark side. This way of hoping can drag us down and keep us from moving on. Imagine a terrible storm has hit you and you have suffered a major loss as a result. However, there is a slight possibility that it could still turn out well, that the loss might come back and be restored. Thus, you still have some hope. You have a belief, an *expectation* that a positive outcome could occur. So what is bad about this situation? What is bad about having hope? It can become a bad situation if that hope is never realized. It can leave you grieving for an extended period of time.

Take two women whose husbands go off to war. One dies and his body is returned home. The other husband goes missing in action. His wife does not know if he is dead or a prisoner of war. Years go by and the more time that goes on, the more she logically knows that he is probably dead. Yet, she hopes he might still be alive and come home any day. Part of her started grieving as soon as she found out he was missing. However, the other part holds out hope for his return.

The first woman whose husband clearly died grieves right away also. However, she then starts to move on, taking those first steps toward resolution and acceptance. Compare this to the second woman. She cannot start to move on. She cannot work toward acceptance. How can anyone accept what is not final? She ends up being stuck in a more depressing place than the first woman for a much longer time, all because she has a little hope. Sure, if that hope is realized, and her husband returns, then it pays off, and she is happier. However, if she doesn't get the desired outcome, she is much worse off.

This is a clear example, but you must question your own situation. Could it be the same thing? Do you have just a little bit of hope? Do you believe that your love might come back to you, your illness could go into remission, or you could get a promotion or a better job? If these things do happen, great! You will be happy. And maybe it is possible and you should hold out hope. But what if it is not likely to happen and you miss out on life, on other opportunities, and live in sadness unnecessarily for years? It is a risky gamble to keep on hoping against all odds. You are betting with your heart.

Hopeless Hope

Some hopes, however, are truly hopeless; yet, they still haunt us. Do you have the hope, the expectation, that your son might come back from the dead? The big problem is that some hopes may be entirely irrational. We know logically that some things are impossible, or very highly improbable. But our hearts hold on to them, nonetheless. Are you stuck in a perpetual grieving process?

I knew my mother was gone. There she was, in a coma, brain dead, body dying. Yet, I asked for a miracle. I thought the doctors were wrong. I bargained with God. And this didn't stop after she was pronounced dead officially. It went on for several weeks. The thoughts and schemes of my mind searched and searched for some way out. Maybe if I could figure out why the stroke happened, I could somehow go back in time and fix it.

My reaction and thoughts were typical in this type of scenario in which a loved one dies suddenly, or where any significant loss occurs in our lives. It just hit me now as I am writing this—am I working with stroke patients in my daily career as a way of somehow fixing my mother and bringing her back? (written with a tear in my eye).

Peace comes from letting go of hope. I know. That sentence does not seem to make sense at first. If your hope is unrealistic, or improbable, it is dark and dragging you down. It is a ball and chain around you. It is keeping you from accepting the truth that you will not get your way in this one. You must accept what you cannot change and move on. While part of you would be devastated by giving up this hope, another part of you will be free to pursue new dreams. So why are you still fighting it? Why are you fighting the call to give up hope?

As long as there is hope then there is at least a chance. Give up that little bit of hope and you give up that little bit of a chance of getting what you want. In your mind, you cannot fathom a world where there is no chance of getting your hope to come true, to get back what you lost. You have to keep trying, no matter how low the odds, as long as there is still a chance. A life without any possibility is not one you can tolerate right now.

Maybe you are just not ready to move on. Maybe it still hurts too much to consider letting go of the hope you have. And that is okay too … for now.

Chapter Takeaways

1. Any significant loss results in grieving
2. Allow yourself time to be sad for a period
3. Possible hope is good.
4. Unrealistic hope can lead us into even more despair

Chapter 5

Accept What You Cannot Change

"But one thing I do: forgetting what is behind and straining toward what is ahead" (Philippians 3:13).

What losses have you suffered in your storm? You have realized after the last chapter that we grieve for any loss, not just those of loved ones who have passed. But what does the word *loss* actually mean? It is imperative that you truly understand this word on a deep level. Of course, this seems like a simple word, but there is more to it.

A *loss* means you no longer have possession of something. You have lost it, as in, it is gone ... gone ... gone for good. Done. You already know this, of course, at least, logically. Or should I more accurately say that part of you knows this? Another part of you does not get it and thinks that maybe, possibly, someday, somehow, you might get it back again. Remember CBT. We have many contradictory and unhelpful thoughts, and we must identify them.

As we just learned from the dark side of hope, your heart might not get what loss truly means. You may know rationally that you need to let it go, that your loss is truly gone for good. But your heart can be stupid. Your heart can still hold on, believing what you lost can somehow come back, even though you know it's truly gone. Deep inside, you may still be asking yourself how you can actually get it back again.

Suffering a severe loss of anything significant is just like suffering the loss of a loved one. We know we have to grieve the death of a loved one. Likewise, we must grieve these other losses as well. But what is the end goal of grieving? The answer is that grieving is a process of learning to *accept*. You have to fully and unequivocally accept the loss. You must fully accept you have indeed **lost** what you wanted.

Serenity Prayer
"God grant me the serenity to accept the things I cannot change, the courage to change the things I can, and the wisdom to know the difference."—Reinhold Niebuhr

I used to get very annoyed hearing this prayer. It just reeked of over used clichés with no real meaning. However, when I started working with the elderly in nursing homes, I began to observe something interesting. In my opinion, this is the most important aspect of moving forward after a storm: *accept what you cannot change.*

I learned this through my work. In the medical and psychological scientific fields of study, we tend to examine the sick and hurting. But we can also learn a great deal from the people who are doing well with their ability to cope. I got to know the strong, emotionally healthy people. I would see somebody in one of my facilities with some type of physical infirmity, for example, someone with a double leg amputation. This person would be in pain, with no friends or family visits, and yet would always go around laughing, smiling, and joking!

I would ask them what their secret was. The answers I would invariably get were all some variant of "Well, I could be upset, but it wouldn't do any good." Sometimes they looked at me as if it was a stupid question and common sense should tell me why. They often say, "Well, what else can a person do?" I would laugh and respond, "You have lots of choices. You can pout and be depressed or get angry. It would not do any good, of course, but you could do those things."

The key to the serenity prayer is the first part—the acceptance that you cannot change some things. Indeed, I have truly come to believe that acceptance is the most important difference between my patients who cope better with terrible situations and those who do not. Acceptance. Acceptance. Acceptance. Accepting that what is lost is actually lost.

Acceptance Does Not Mean Liking
Acceptance does not mean that you like what has happened. Not at all! I have had numerous clients, friends, and family, object to this advice because they get these two concepts confused. No one expects you to be happy when you have experienced a loss. You can keep feeling sad and frustrated. I am not trying to talk you out of feeling miserable. This is just a matter of looking at the facts, and gaining a perspective that can help.

Can your loss be retrieved? Can the situation be reversed? If the facts say no, then accept it. Plain and simple. Getting your heart to understand that will take more time, but start with your logical head, fully admitting the situation will not change.

There is a great older expression: "It's like beating a dead horse." This is a beautifully simple but poignant analogy that can make us laugh at how silly our reasoning can be when we are depressed. When you have a hard time moving on from a storm, when it is difficult to let go and accept, it is as if you are beating this dead horse, trying to get it to run.

You have thoughts that if you could just kick the horse the right way, it might go. Maybe if you pet it the right way … maybe if you beat it with the right stick... maybe if you put a carrot in front of it ... then just maybe you could get it to run, maybe. It is at least worth a shot, right? But—*it cannot run*! It is dead! Why are you still trying to get it to move? That is a powerful illustration of how pointless our thinking and actions can be when we refuse to accept the reality of a situation. We all think like this at times. Can you consider the possibility that this is how your mind is working?

Let us look at a typical storm situation as an example. Your boyfriend just broke up with you and your heart is crushed. It is not what you want. You still want to be with him. It is a big loss for you. You are grieving this loss and your heart is having a hard time accepting it. You start thinking about all the reasons why he might have been unhappy with you. You think that maybe you could still be with him if only… if only you were prettier, had longer hair, did not nag him about his job, and/or, the standard, maybe if you were thinner. You try to figure out what the problem is because if you can get that part right, you might get him back again. You come up with all kinds of ideas to try to get him back. You start calling him, leaving messages. You tell him the things you think he wants to hear. You go on a crash diet and dye your hair. You make him promises. You try to tell his friends about how he should give you another chance.

Maybe you are not doing anything directly to try to get him back, but you are obsessively analyzing the situation, trying to figure out where the relationship went bad, what he did wrong, and what you did wrong. You pray to God to bring him back. However, these are all just different ways to get the dead horse to run. These are attempts to get what is dead moving again. You have not accepted it is lost; it is over. As a result, you keep yourself chained and imprisoned by the overwhelming sadness. The quality of your life is worse and continues to be bad for a much longer time than is necessary.

Giving Up the Cookie
Another good illustration of accepting what we cannot change that I like to use is one of a little girl who asks her mother for a cookie before dinner. Your storms are so much more important than a little girl's cookie. But this analogy proves a point because to that little girl, the cookie is everything! The loss you have endured may have been truly terrible, but there is still something you could learn through this.

A good mom will say no to her beloved little girl because the cookie will ruin her appetite and fill her up with empty calories. After Mom says no, the child throws a big, screaming, flailing temper tantrum, crying and all, hoping to persuade her mom to give her the cookie, to get her way.

It is not just that the little girl will not get her way with the cookie, but she will also suffer in two additional ways. The girl will pay the emotional price of being depressed or angry for a while. But she will also miss out on the playtime she usually has before dinner because she is spending it crying. After dinner, it is time for her bedtime routine and to sleep. She is upset once she realizes she missed out on playtime, which makes her even more depressed.

Compare this to how other kids could handle the same situation. They too will be sad but will give up their attempts to get the cookie because they know *and accept* it is a losing battle. They will accept they will not get that cookie and go on playing, still sad but enjoying life.

At times, we are all like this little girl who throws a temper tantrum! Most of us have a little bit of that girl in us, and we never fully grow out of it. We just learn to throw more sophisticated, and/or passive-aggressive temper tantrums. We spend so much of our time pouting, crying, and being upset, instead of living life, all because we are upset about not getting our way. I like that phrase, "not getting our way." At first, it seems like a very child-like and immature way of referring to our problems. Yet, I think it accurately describes how we honestly think deep inside. We usually utilize more sophisticated methods of throwing temper tantrums—well, most of us, anyway. I know some who still look like four-year-olds, becoming angry and violent. I have even had to use the techniques in this book for court-ordered anger management classes for some of these people.

Most of the time, we do not look as if we are throwing temper tantrums at others, but on the inside, we are. Many little kids pout as do many adults. I am often guilty of this myself. But flat-out depression can be our temper tantrums too. As previously explained, we sometimes want to get depressed to get our way.

We may also end up acting in a passive-aggressive manner against something, someone, or even ourselves. A little cookieless girl is mad and resentful toward her mother. You may be irritable toward your loved ones, taking your anger out on them. Or you rebel against yourself, drinking heavily, using drugs, having dangerous casual sex, or over-eating.

But your desired object may not be a luxury in life like a cookie. What you want may be a good and natural thing to desire and it is understandable you are upset about losing it, for example, a job, friend, home, independence, and, especially love. We refuse to give in to not getting our way, because "our way" is a normal thing we usually expect to get in life. You may not be going through such a hard time if you just wanted something trivial. However, the same concept of acceptance still applies. You will not get your loved one, your health back, or your job back. You have *lost* them. So why throw a temper tantrum? That behavior will not get back what was lost. It is over; accept that it is gone.

The important thing about this illustration is you must first recognize when you are throwing a temper tantrum, whether it is a violent outburst, depression, or self-destructive behavior. Once you can admit you are having a temper tantrum because you did not get your way, you did not get your cookie, you can better accept that Mom (the storm) said no and you will not get your cookie, no matter how good or normal it is to desire it.

Chapter Takeaways

1. Accept what you cannot change. Accept that what is lost is lost.
2. Acceptance does not mean what happened was right.
3. What is the cookie you want? Do not throw a temper tantrum if you do not get it.

Chapter 6

Dangers of Selfishness

"For where you have envy and selfish ambition, there you find disorder and every evil practice" (James 3:16).

Ironically, there are many ways we can attempt to be happier that might be making us unhappier. I have discovered that selfish people are seldom very happy, even though they are always fighting for their happiness. On the other hand, unselfish people are not so concerned with their happiness; yet, they are often happy. Are you willing to take another hard look at yourself and see if selfishness could be stopping you from surviving your storm?

Many people are more selfish, or self-centered than they realize. Moreover, depression can make people selfish. Depression makes us much more self-centered and selfish than usual. This is a normal defense mechanism, especially during a life storm. You have been emotionally hurt. So naturally, you will be afraid of being hurt more. When we are happy, it is easier to go out and give to others. However, the act of giving puts us in a more vulnerable position. We might be able to handle that when we are well. But we cannot handle it emotionally when we are hurt.

While this defensive posture is normal and understandable in a stressful situation, it is not a good attitude. Furthermore, it will not help you survive the storm and have a better life. As I said earlier, the more depressed we are, the more selfish we become.

But selfish people are never happy. They are always looking for what they did not get, and who did not do what they should have done to make them happy. They blame others for their problems. As we just examined, our minds become much more negative when depressed. So if someone is depressed her narrow focus will only be on herself and she will become increasingly wrapped up in self-pity. You may not normally be a selfish person. But are you being more selfish now because of the storm and depression?

Looking at things selfishly causes a snowballing problem. Depression makes us more selfish. Selfishness naturally leads to negativity. Thinking negatively results in greater depression. It can become a terrible downward cycle. You can never fight your way through a storm with selfishness and negativity. Looking at only the downside of situations has a primary negative consequence of becoming even sadder than you already were. Why do you want to be sadder? Aren't you sad enough already? In addition, thinking more selfishly leads to acting more selfishly, which does not make for good friends and relationships. People do not want to be around others who do not care about anyone but themselves.

Refuse to be selfish. On the surface, it makes sense to look out for yourself. But a deeper look reveals this is ironically self-destructive. When you are depressed and only look inward, it is easy to become trapped in a wall of your own self-pity. You might genuinely have a good reason to feel sorry for yourself. And I am all in favor of going through a time of self-pity, having a pity party, and feeling sorry for yourself. I often prescribed for my patients to feel sorry for themselves. But just for a short time! You do this purposely, knowing you will not stay in that state forever. The time will come when you must stop the pity party, put on your big girl panties, look outside yourself and see others.

One of the best treatments for people who are severely depressed is getting them to think outside of themselves and be more compassionate. Pets are always good for helping us care for one another. They have to be fed and cared for and, of course, in return, they provide unconditional love. However, ideally, caring for other people is even better than for pets when it comes to pushing us to feel better about ourselves. Indeed, it takes more work to do this for humans and there is more potential for rejection, but it's much more rewarding when it works out. When you start concerning yourself with other people, you stop worrying so much about yourself, you feel good because you are helping someone else, and lo and behold, the depression gets better.

You have now started a positive cycle of thoughts. As you start to feel better about yourself, you open your eyes to the other bits of information that show you life has good parts to it and that there is hope. You then feel better and start doing more things. Consequently, you think and feel better. So remember the irony that people who only focus on their happiness are less happy, and people who do not focus on their happiness but instead focus on others' happiness are happier.

Are You a Mean Person?
Have you noticed that mean people never seem happy? We all know several of them. They are cold, distant, grumpy, complaining, and negative. They seem to have a chip on their shoulders. They expect everyone in their world to make them happy...or else.

Why are they mean, selfish, unloving, and ultimately so unhappy? To them, their lives are not as they should be. Life has not been fair and they have been victimized or traumatized. It is one thing to seek happiness, but it is another thing altogether to demand it from life and everyone around you.

So one theory: a storm makes you feel depressed, which causes you to withdraw from life and retreat. Being isolated, your attention is focused on yourself primarily. This causes further selfishness and meanness. This very well could be the true causal pattern. However, could it be the other way around? Maybe meanness and self-centeredness are causing depression. Having a negative attitude about life can taint everything. Mean people are not just mean to others, but also themselves, the future, and everything. Instead of looking through rose-colored glasses, it is more like brown-colored glasses. Everything is dull and lifeless. There is no joy or hope. Only anger exists. Anger toward others and themselves. All they think about is how life has not given them what they wanted and it is not fair!

The origins of how their personality developed can vary greatly. Some deserve more sympathy than others. Some have truly had bad childhoods and have become callous toward life as a result. However, some mean people had great lives and were simply just spoiled. Maybe they did not grow up with money at all, but their parents were just too lazy to discipline them properly. Some parents want to be their children's friends more than their parents and cannot bear to see their children upset. Unfortunately, this is not an uncommon scenario. Trust me; my early psychology years were spent trying to teach parenting skills to parents who did not care enough to try to teach their kids to be better people and think of others more than themselves. Children who have not been properly disciplined grow up to be mean and unhappy adults.

Are you a mean person? You may not even realize it if you are, but you just might be. It is a sad fact that most mean people do not think of themselves as being the problem. I know some of the key people in my life were mean a great deal of the time, but they thought of themselves as the victims.

Maybe you are not a bad person overall, but you are mean at times in certain situations. Maybe you have become colder and more self-protective. Have you become more defensive, cold, distant, grumpy, self-absorbed, and mean because of the sadness, hurt, and disappointment you feel? And how is that working for you? It may keep you from getting hurt as much, but it will not make you happy!

"Happiness is like a butterfly; the more you chase it, the more it will elude you, but if you turn your attention to other things, it will come and sit softly on your shoulder."—Thoreau

The more you try to demand happiness from everyone and everything around you, the less content you will be. You will never have enough. You will never be satisfied. Money cannot buy happiness if you don't appreciate the good it brings. Similarly, those with a cold, defensive, angry attitude will never be appeased or content. It does not matter how well they are treated by the people in their lives, they will continue to look at what is wrong, who has wronged them, and how unfair the world is.

In contrast, the people who focus on others' happiness, not on themselves, are usually the happiest. One great therapy idea for those with depression is to get them to volunteer with some charity, for example, a food bank. These clients become more focused on others and more light-hearted and content.

Miller's Irony of Happiness
The more one fights for his own happiness
The less happy he will be.
The less one cares about his own happiness and more about others' The happier he is.

So Shouldn't I Try to Be Happy?
Now, the problem is not the pursuit of your pleasure. Nothing is necessarily wrong or sinful about wanting to be happy

and trying to find happiness. Throughout the Bible, God demonstrated that He knows how we are made. He knows we seek our best interests. After all, He made us.

Think about the strategies He used to motivate us. He entices us with the wonderfulness of His love and, especially with how nice heaven will be. He also uses the threat of hell and loss of His fellowship to warn us, indeed, to scare us in order to keep us from hurting. It is easy. Do you want to be happy? Follow God and His ways. Yes, His love is so extraordinary to us. He has done everything He can do to bring us to Him and make us happy. But we have the choice to love Him or not, to be happy with ourselves or not. If this is God's method, then it is obvious that He knows we are seeking our own pleasure. Therefore, it is okay to want to be happy!

"Every man, whatsoever his condition, desires to be happy."—Saint Augustine

This is not to imply it is ever okay to hurt others or ignore them in our pursuit of pleasure. The selfish pursuit of pleasure at the expense of others is never encouraged. The problem is not that we seek happiness. The problem is the things we seek pleasure in. We seek pleasure in superficial, short-term fleshly things that do not last. Instead, we should seek the deeper things that bring us pure joy now and in the long-term future. We were made to give others love, and, in doing so, ideally, this giving makes us truly happy. We were made to be happy by serving God and others. When we look back at our lives, we usually find in the long run, we were happiest when we were doing what God wanted us to do. Even if we are miserable and must sacrifice for someone else's happiness, we can gain contentment knowing we are at least doing the right thing.

Yes, sometimes people take advantage of our generosity and show no appreciation. Naturally, this makes us sad. The truth is we all need acknowledgment sometimes. Even the most unselfish people will get tired of giving all the time, while others just take it for granted. There are many marriages in which one party keeps giving and the other just keeps taking and treating the spouse worse and worse as time goes on. It is only human for this to wear away at someone after a while.

Indeed, we should be good, for goodness sake, for God's sake, and our own sake. However, I am not talking about being good to earn Brownie points for God. That thinking does not get you into heaven anyway. "It is only by faith we are saved anyway, not as a result of Brownie's points, so that no one can boast" (Ephesians 2:8 Monte's version). Thus, this strategy to be happier is not based on what we *should* do religiously to be happy. It is also not based on arbitrary rules, but on what actually works to make us happy. God made us for love. When we love God and others before we love ourselves, we end up being happier.

Does It Make You Happy to Make Me Happy
Even if you can honestly say you are not a mean person, you still have to examine where your focus is. Are you overly focused on yourself or others? I realized a while back that it made me happy to make others happy. I loved making my daughter breakfast every weekend morning, reading to her

every night, and just hanging out with her all the time. I enjoyed getting up and taking care of my wife, giving her back rubs most nights, and making her breakfast in bed. I looked at other people. We all know simple and humble people with servants' hearts who are sincerely happy. It makes a mother happy to see her family enjoying her dinner and a dad happy to provide well for his family.

However, I also learned the hard way that some do not seem to understand this concept at all. We talked about mean people already. While some people may not exactly be mean, they may be very self-centered, and/or selfish. I know several people who do not have a mean bone in their bodies. However, they do not think about others much. They live for themselves. They are in their own little worlds. These people may do something nice for others at times, maybe even often, but it is not their motivation. Making others happy does not inspire them to focus more on others and their happiness.

The problem is that those who do not get a thrill from helping others tend to be unhappy. Mean people are obviously unhappy. Those who are self-focused are also less happy than unselfish people. They are probably not nearly as bad as the mean ones, but yes, they are less likely to find the ultimate happiness they seek.

Knowing someone else is feeling better because of our actions, gives us a sense of purpose and meaning. As said before, we were made by God to love others, not just to feel love for them, but to actively give love to them. It is only when things go wrong that this gets messed up inside so many of us.

My old folks in the homes have gone through, and are still going through severe storms. A useful strategy I have used with them is to get them to help some of the other patients who live there. This helpful behavior might only be to get them to talk to a few of the little old ladies and tell them they look nice. Or it may be something more important like starting a Bible study.

One of the many losses these seniors have had to endure is the loss of a sense of purpose. A mother has no children or young grandchildren to take care of. A man cannot build, repair, or fix anything. In the nursing homes, there are no gardens to tend, houses to clean, or even shopping to do. I try to help them realize God might still have a purpose for them by helping others who are more in need. I try to get them to see that even the simplest of acts can make someone's day.

One of my favorite stories in my nursing home is of the little man with severe cerebral palsy. Here was a 70-year-old man, who was not even four feet tall if you could have stretched him out. He was in an electric wheelchair and was never able to walk for a day in his life. You could not understand everything he said. He had a simple mind, maybe just a little bit smarter technically than someone with mental retardation. He also had severe COPD with severe attacks where he could barely breathe before getting another breathing treatment. He would zoom around the facility in that thing smiling, talking to everyone, especially about Jesus. Sure, he was a flirt, but he was friendly and respectful to all. When he passed, I went to his funeral and the tiny little Baptist church was packed with numerous people getting up to tell about how much this man meant to them.

Here is a guy who was severely physically handicapped, could not speak well, and was of simple intelligence. Yet, he served a purpose. He allowed himself to be used by God powerfully, even with his very limited resources. This little man used the little bit God gave him and multiplied it greatly!

Jesus told a parable about talents in Matthew 25:14. He gave three servants money to manage. Two managed their portions well but one did not. This little, big man was given a little bit but made the most of what he was given. I always love it when my clients, whom I am trying to minister to, end up ministering to me.

This man endured one life storm after another after another. He had every right to be depressed, angry, resentful, and to feel useless and worthless. However, he was not caught up in self-pity and loathing. Instead, he found joy. He found joy by giving and focusing on Christ and others.

You may not be a mean, selfish person. But are you a thoughtful person, one who will try to find how to help others? If not, you can always learn to be. This is about your happiness. I want you to be happy. You will find yourself being happier if you can learn how to be happy by making others happy.

Chapter Takeaways

1. Be aware of how it is common to become more subtly selfish when depressed and in a storm
2. Selfishness leads to more depression
3. Selfishness can lead to hurting others
4. Focus on helping others to improve your depression
5. Seek your own happiness, but do so with a loving heart toward others

Chapter 7

Are Your Expectations Too High?

"For where you have envy and selfish ambition, there you find disorder and every evil practice" (James 3:16).

Let us go back to the roses and thorns analogy. The analogy was used earlier to point out how we have choices to make about how we view our lives. Now, I want to use the roses and thorns to talk about what we expect out of life and how these expectations greatly affect our ability to cope with storms. So I ask the key question again, do you expect life to be full of roses, and how dare there be thorns, or do you expect life to be full of thorns and thank God for the roses?

Some pop psychology theories say the word "should" is a word we *should* never use. This is an overly simplistic rule, of course. The thinking is that we shouldn't expect or assume too much out of life. However, we *should* take a look at our use of our *shoulds*. We all have expectations. We cannot run from them. We will have them and specific ones for every aspect of our lives. The question isn't whether or not we should think about our *shoulds*. The question is what are our specific *shoulds*, and are they helping us?

So what do you expect your life *should* be like? "Should" is a dangerous word. It holds a great deal of power in our lives, although in a very subtle manner. It is all about the expectations we set up for ourselves. Our *shoulds* set the bar for the minimum quality of our lives, which we *think* we need to achieve for us to be happy. Like it or not, we have a lot of *shoulds* in our minds. "Life *should* be fair." "I *should* be healthy." "He *should* love me." "I *should* be happy." However, maybe what is getting you down is that your *shoulds*—your expectations—are too unrealistic, even ones that may seem nice and normal. Sometimes you have to lower your *shoulds* because they are set too high from the start. However, sometimes it is not that simple, and your situation, your storm, makes it much harder to cope. Sometimes when tragedy strikes, you must lower your expectations because you have to accept the situation will not get any better, and you then have a choice to deal with it as it is or leave it.

It is imperative that you openly express what your specific expectations are. We spoke earlier about how you have to figure out your specific thoughts before you can understand how they are affecting your emotions and behaviors. Right now, you need to look specifically at your thoughts around your expectations. They can be very subtle and difficult to uncover, even though it is your brain that believes them. You may not be aware of many of them. You certainly have not usually articulated the majority out loud. Many of your thoughts and expectations may be irrational, unrealistic, and even silly. You may not even want to admit to yourself that you have some of these thoughts. You may be ashamed to admit that your expectations can be quite selfish. But to use this way of thinking to help you cope with your life, you may have to take a hard look at your expectations and be willing to change them.

Expectations in the Form of Math

I like to see things mapped out for myself to help me better understand the concept. If you do not like math, that's okay! This is easier than that. To change and grow, you must start viewing your problems in a new way. It often helps to see your problems laid out in front of you.

Take any one area in your life. For example, take the problem area of your life, maybe the storm in your life that caused you to read this book in the first place. You believe your life in this area *should* be at least of a certain quality. Now imagine putting some type of quantitative value on how well that is working out for you. If that value is lower than the bar you have set up (your *should*), then you are unhappy, sad, angry, and afraid. Think of this as a math equation. If your life situation is of greater value than your expectations then you are happy. Of course, the converse of this is true as well.

If Life ≥ Expectations = Happy
If your Quality of Life is greater than or equal to your Expectations then this results in you being Happy

HOWEVER

If Life < Expectations = Sad, Angry, Scared
If your Quality of Life is less than your Expectations then you are either Sad, Angry, or Scared

I know it is difficult to put a numerical value on the quality of the different areas of your life, but, in a way, your mind is already doing just this. So, let's say in one area, life is giving you a score of 6 (on a scale of 1 to 10), and you expected at least a 5 then the result is that you are content in this area. As an example, if you think your job satisfaction *should* be at least a 7 and it ends up being a 5, then you are not happy or fulfilled in that job.

We want our life circumstances to work out well and to meet our expectations. However, for one reason or another, many areas of life do not meet our expectations. As we have learned, we do not have control over some things in our life. So, if that is the case, and you cannot change the situation, then maybe you will have to change the other part of the equation and lower your expectations in order to be happier, or sometimes, just less miserable, to be honest.

The good news is that ultimately, you have some control over how you feel based on this simple way of looking at it. That is, you have control over how you choose to see your situation. You can choose your level of expectation. You can control that! I made the case earlier that ultimately, though difficult to do, you can control your own happiness. Of course, it is not that simple, but the point is, you can. You need to closely examine your expectations. The reality is if your expectations are lower, then life would be relatively better than you expected and you would be happier.

At times, it is wise to lower the bar—to lower your expectations. Stay with me here and let us explore this concept. I understand it does not sound very encouraging to hear someone suggest you lower your expectations, but this way, you may have much more peace.

Unrealistic Expectations

Have you considered your expectations may have been too high and unrealistic in the first place? I am not saying if you are unhappy then your expectations must be too high. Your expectations might be totally understandable and typical. You may not be asking for more than anyone else would in your situation. We will deal with that situation in a minute. But maybe you do want too much.

Men often watch easily attainable pornography and can get the impression that all women should be perfectly built and want sex all the time. However, make no mistake, women enjoy pornography every bit just as much as men, even with the kids in the room. Hollywood movies and television, along with romance novels, give women a false sense of how husbands should act, just as much as pornography can for men. The ruggedly handsome man in movies is articulate with his thoughts and feelings and ends up giving it all up to confess his love to his soulmate. "Oh, if only my husband loved me that much." Sigh. Maybe you expect to have the perfect job that pays you well and gives you a sense of fulfillment and respect. After all, you paid your $150,000 for a four-year college degree.

I know many social workers who thought they were going to save the world. But they find themselves fighting against government bureaucracies and systems and paperwork that tie their hands from doing much actual good. So, yes, sometimes we have to take a sincere look at our expectations and realize they were never realistic.

Perhaps you have already been doing this in some areas of your life effectively, but you just weren't aware you were doing it. Let us apply that natural strategy more purposefully to the problem area of your life. To demonstrate how many of us are already healthily lowering our expectations, just look at the common marriage.

When we first get married, we expect it to be near perfect, so our expectation score would be a 9 on a scale of 1 to 10. As marriage goes on, the reality of life and love causes most of us to lower that to a 7 or so. We figure out that our spouses will not love us as much as they did when dating. Moreover, the stress of life gets in the way of an idealistic blissful eternal honeymoon, and we realize that this is okay! We all have to adapt to our environments or else, we would go crazy.

I am a pretty easygoing guy, but I hate driving through town—the rush hour traffic, slow drivers in the fast lane, and jerks cutting you off. So I would get frustrated and very irritated when driving to and from work. However, I took my own advice and started to *expect* bad traffic and idiot drivers. When someone cuts me off, I just pull back and say, "Hey, there's today's idiot!" Or, I expect a traffic jam, maybe even the kind that exists for no other reason than rubberneckers looking at the wreck on the other side of the highway. Thus, I am still content, even though it is going to take me over an hour to get home. Life is normally much harder than this, of course, but, the concept is still the same.

Aim Lower?

Okay, but what if your situation is much worse than this? Maybe your expectations are not too high in a typical situation. You just want a normal life, a content life, not anything great; yet, that is not even close to what your life has become. How can you try to find a way to manage your emotions and survive emotionally? When difficult problems arise in your life that you cannot change, is your expectation bar set too high? I hate saying this. On one hand, your expectations are realistic. But given the situation, it is no longer realistic to expect things to turn out as you want.

You must lower your expectations. In our math equations, the number of how good your life is in that area will be lower than the expectation and obviously, you will be disappointed. You know you cannot change one side of the equation, so you must change your expectations. Okay, you can just resign yourself to being depressed, but this would be your choice. It is also your choice to lower the expectation.

Then there are storms that suddenly appear on the horizon. Of course, we never *expect* a storm of life to hit. When death strikes, when you catch your lover cheating on you, when you lose your job, when your child gets diagnosed with a serious disease—these things automatically mean your expectations of happiness in that area of your life will not be met at all. No one can blame a 50-year-old husband and father for being depressed about having a serious new health problem such as a stroke. Likewise, no one would say a good wife, whose husband just left her, does not have the right to be heartbroken. Terrible storms will hurt us a great deal;

there's no doubt about it. However, life must still go on after a storm.

Now I know what you are yelling. "But I don't *want* to lower my expectations!" I know. You should not have to if they were realistic, to begin with. I know it's not an easy thing that I am asking you to do. Like accepting the reality of a loss when you are grieving, this is not a way of thinking that you can come to very quickly. However, you can learn to change your outlook on the situation. You must if you want to survive tough situations. It is not ideal. It is not fair. You want to pout. You want to scream. But in the life happiness equation, your situational score cannot change. So you can only live with sadness, anger, or anxiety, or decide to lower your expectations and go on with your life. You have a choice.

My doctoral dissertation looked at how some women (not most, but some) can be content even when their husbands are cheating. I guess their expectation for a good enough marriage is fairly low, maybe around a four. Regardless of how low a person can go and be content, this demonstrates how most of us already have been lowering our expectations to be happier.

Aim Higher?
Up to this point, I have been pushing you to take a difficult look at yourself and lower your expectations. However, there are times in our lives when we *should not* lower our expectations any further. In some situations, it is a good thing to set the bar high and to have high expectations. Of course, you must

aim high when you are young in regard to your career or ministry goals, and in your desire to have a decent spouse. We all push our kids to dream big and do what they can to achieve those goals. It is good to value yourself without being prideful and to believe you do not have to put up with a bunch of garbage.

I have a patient in one of my nursing homes who came from a poor part of Detroit. She never had more than a minimum wage job and put up with an abusive, alcoholic husband for years. Her expectation bar was set way too low. As I got to know her better, I realized how very intelligent she was. She would notice things and ask very deep questions. However, she was taught that her opinions and happiness never mattered and that she wasn't bright enough to have her own opinion. She knew she was loved by Jesus, and this certainly helped her to have a humble attitude toward herself. I started pointing out the many ways that she was more intelligent than average, but she would not believe me at first. It has taken me a few years to do it, but she is now seeing that she is indeed an intelligent and valuable woman. She *should* have had higher expectations for her life, but others around her taught her not to do so.

If you are in a relationship, then you *should* absolutely *expect* a certain amount of respect. You should *expect* not to be physically hurt. If you have a job, you should expect not to have to put up with sexual harassment to keep your job. If you want to have friends, you should *expect* that they will not backstab you or pressure you to do things you are not comfortable doing.

Change the Things You Can

But why is it healthy to expect more in these situations compared to other situations when I'm asking you to lower your expectations? How should you know when to lower and when to raise? A key determination in knowing when to do what goes back to a key point I made earlier —The Serenity Prayer. Yes, we must accept what we cannot change, but we also have to change the things we can. In counseling, I tend to focus on the accepting part, since we cannot change so many problems and storms in our lives. However, the second part of the prayer is also very important. We must have the *courage* to change the things we can change. It takes a lot of courage to change our lives.

A woman who finds herself in an abusive relationship has to muster up a great deal of courage to leave and start a new life. Leaving a job, starting a new career, or launching your own business can all be very scary and takes a lot of courage.

I have written an entire book on helping women get out of abusive relationships. I can tell you that the psychological roadblocks in the way of women getting out from under the thumb of an abuser can be quite extensive! They are too many and some are too complex to get into here. But changing your situation instead of your expectation is the best option to weather this terrible, abusive storm. It can be extremely difficult to gather the courage to change that.

Another look at our Expectation Equation is needed to summarize this difference. When a storm of life hits, our Life score is less than our Expectations and we suffer negative results. We then have three, and only three choices. You *have to* do one of the following:

1. Change the things you can change, thus, improving your Quality of Life—and be content.
2. Accept the things you cannot change and lower your Expectations—and be content.
3. Feel sorry for yourself and just feel Sad, Angry, or Afraid indefinitely.

If Life ≤ Expectations = Sad, Angry, Afraid

Change Life, Change Expectations, or Settle for negative feelings.

That is all. You cannot escape this. In each one of your life's struggles, you have already been choosing one of these three. I am sure that you have picked each one in different circumstances. My goal here is to teach you that you have a choice. In any storm or disappointment of life, you can choose the first two options and be more content. Again, being content is not ideal. It is not at all feeling as happy as you would want, but feeling happy enough.

The third choice is not the best, though still a choice. We talked about how when grieving you want to be sad, at least, for a while. There are more complex reasons that I have tried to analyze about why one would want to feel bad, though we may not realize it. A big task of mine is to get you to look at yourself on a deeper level. If you are not choosing to be more content, then you are choosing to be upset. If this is the case, then own it. Although, if this is the case, you will have to admit that your unhappiness was your choice at this point. Yes, you didn't cause it initially, but you did play a part in rejecting a path for more contentment.

Overall Life Expectations

Up to this point, we have been looking at specific individual areas of your life and the expectations that dictate your level of happiness in those areas. But we also have a global view of our happiness, in which we look at all the areas of our lives combined. We all have some aspects of our lives that are better than others, and some that are worse. Given this, how do we evaluate our overall happiness, looking at all of the areas, not just one?

Here are some main categories in our lives that we could differentiate as separate categories:

Romance	Family	Friends	Career/Money
Health	Hobbies	Spirituality	

Our lives can be divided, or even subdivided differently than I did here. For instance, your relationship with your children will be different from that with your siblings. And even the romantic part of life can be divided. For example, I may be happy with the friendship area of the marriage but not the sexual part. For our purposes here, it isn't important how you break down your life. However, it is vital to understand that subconsciously, you have already been breaking your life into categories.

There is no universal or correct way to look at your overall happiness. Some people expect all of the areas of your life to be at, or above, the individual expected level to be globally happy. Some just need more areas in the positive range than in the negative. However, most of us tend to take the approach of valuing some of these areas more than others. When we look at life in this manner, we will be content, as long as the primary areas of our lives are good, even if all the other ones are sub-par.

Overall, there are three possible views of global happiness. "I will be content with my life if":

1. All areas of my life meet expectations.
2. More areas meet expectations than those that do not.
3. The primary areas of my life meet expectations.

So how are you looking at your life? What do you expect out of your life? What *should* your life look like? Just as with individual expectations, your views may or may not be realistic or helpful. Rather, they may need to be reevaluated if you want to be more content. I pointed out that we can all choose to break our lives down into different categories and subcategories. We can also choose for ourselves what method we use to gauge our overall happiness. Well, if we can choose how we look at our lives, then we can also choose to look at them differently if we want to cope and be more content.

If you believe that **all** areas have to meet expectations, then I hate to say it, but you are probably being unrealistic. Needless to say, we *want* all areas of our lives to meet expectations.

However, life is probably going to let you down in some areas. Life usually stinks like that. Or, you are going to mess up in one or several areas of your life. Let us go back to our primary quote for this chapter. Are you unhappy with your whole life if there are just one or two thorns in your rose bush?

In contrast, the second approach of only needing more areas that are good than there are that are bad is a much more realistic viewpoint. Certainly, no one measures out each area, then calculates the grand total to see if more areas are in the positive range. This is a ballpark estimate. However, in this viewpoint, you generally *expect* and accept that life is not going to be perfect, or close to perfect.

Are you focusing on the negative and not the positive? We have looked at how useful it is to be thankful for what is good in your life (the roses) and not just look at what is bad (the thorns). Let's apply this positivity toward this perspective of looking at the big areas of your life. It is not helpful for you to just feel sorry for yourself for the areas of your life that are bad. You need to appreciate that some areas are good.

Chapter Takeaways

1. Articulate your expectations. What are your "shoulds"?
2. Do you expect life to be easy or hard?
3. Know when to lower expectations because they are unrealistic.

4. Know when to stand firm on your expectations or even raise them.
5. If expectations are realistic, then change the situation to meet them. Or accept your situation as it is and move on. That, or just feel sorry for yourself.
6. Examine expectations in all areas of your life.

Chapter 8

How to Apply Gratitude

"And the peace of God, which surpasses all understanding, will guard your hearts and minds through Christ Jesus" (Philippians 4:7).

The peace that passes understanding. These words are often heard, especially in church circles. It talks about having peace even when it does not make sense to have peace, given one's circumstances. It is suggesting that we can have severe life storms; yet, we can still be content, even though it would be understandable to be miserable.

The above verse is often used to give us hope and get us through troubled times. But the problem is it does not tell us how. How do I get this peace? I need more help than a nice little saying. I hate overused clichés, especially when they sound too churchy. Okay, I know I need to lean on God more to help me with this, but how? Give me some real, practical, everyday advice on how to make this real for my life.

Let's look at the bigger context around that verse and see if we can get some answers.

*"Do not be anxious about anything, but in every situation, by prayer and petition, **with thanksgiving**, present your requests to God.*

And the peace which transcends all understanding, will guard your hearts and your minds in Christ Jesus" (Philippians 4:6, 7 NIV, emphasis added).

I think this verse points out that the secret to that peace is, "with thanksgiving." Paul is not talking about our football and turkey holiday in November. He is making a point that we need to be thankful for the things *we have* and not just feel sorry for ourselves because of what *we do not* have or have lost. What are you going to purposely choose to focus on, the negative or positive? In essence, he is saying we need to appreciate the roses in our lives and not just complain about the thorns. Where have you heard that before?

Again, this is not denying that you have very real problems. That is why the Bible uses the expression, "Peace that passes understanding." The "passes understanding" part is another way of saying, "Anyone in their right mind would be stressed by this!" God knows we are hurting and suffering. He knows that sometimes it is normal and understandable ***not*** to have peace. But He wants you to have peace anyway, despite the chaos of life.

Not Being Thankful
A six-year-old little girl has a wealthy family. Her mother and father love her to death and try to spoil her as much as they can. On Christmas Day, she receives dozens of presents—fancy dolls, a new puppy dog, games, Barbie car, candy. However, after she opens the last one, she is unhappy and starts throwing a fit because she did not get the one doll she was hoping to get. She should be so happy and

appreciative of all she received and how hard her parents worked to give her those things. The little brat!

I know you are hurting. I know the storm you are going through is probably something that any normal person would be sad, anxious, or frustrated about. I do not mean to minimize or belittle your pain. Read through this and think about the broader perspective. But the hard-core truth is we are all this spoiled little girl! We have all been given so much and should be happy with what God has given us and thankful for it, not looking at what we do not have. To be honest, I have to remind myself of this all the time. I am this spoiled girl! I still get upset when I do not get what I want. Even when all I want is for life to be fair, to be normal. But I am that spoiled little girl. I pout and cry when I don't get my way. Are you like this girl at times?

Indeed, life may be extremely unfair for you right now. I really do not want to imply that you are a spoiled girl when your husband loses his job, your health is bad, and you cannot pay the bills. As I have said before, there is a time to feel sorry for yourself, for a bit. However, can you take a step back and examine your life from a bigger perspective? Can you consider your own perspective in this light to learn something that could help you?

The crux of the girl's problem is that she is not thankful. She focused on the things she did not have, not the things she had. Are you like her? What have you been given in your life, compared to what you do not have? Again, this is not saying you do not have a right to be sad or upset when a storm really has hit you. But even then, it still can help immensely to look at all you do have.

In the end, she hurts herself. Compare her to another child who is just happy to have any toys for Christmas. Forget about morals and how one should think. Let's look at the bottom line of what I want for you—to be happy, to have peace! Being thankful makes your life better! You may not get the doll you wanted. You may not even get your spouse, job, or health back, but whatever you are sad about not getting, life is logically better when you are looking at the good that is still in your life.

"I cried because I had no shoes until I met a man who had no feet."—(Helen Keller)

I have to admit, when I am feeling down, there are days when the last thing I want to do is listen to other people's problems all day. However, I go to the nursing home and look at all of the problems those guys have to go through, and how well so many of them get through, and it strengthens me. Sometimes I feel ashamed that I was even feeling sorry for myself at all. I want to complain because of the stress of making my mortgage, but I am talking to a man who lost his nice house of 45 years that was all paid for, only to be in a small room with a stranger who keeps the room too hot and the television on all night. Really? Really? How can I be that self-centered and selfish to feel sorry for myself anywhere near these people?

Three Easy-to-Remember Categories to Help: Past, Present, Future

I know when I am depressed and I think logically that I *should* be thankful, but sometimes all I can ever think about are a few simple things. Do you recall how I talked about how our brains want to think more depressed thoughts when depressed? It is very difficult to get your brain to come up with things to be thankful for, especially when you are hurting and need those positive thoughts the most.

A few years ago, I figured out a way to help myself more easily recall all the good things in my life, to not feel as sorry for myself at times. I categorized things in my life into three easy-to-remember categories based on time: the past, present, and future. What has been good in your life? What is still good in your life (this is often the hardest one)? Then the final category is what will be good in my life later.

Your Past – A Good Life?

Did you have a good life in your past? Surely, you had some good things at several different points in your life. Maybe you had a good upbringing. Maybe you had a good childhood with money, material possessions, and love from your parents. Maybe your life was okay until you arrived at high school and/or college. Maybe it was good in early adulthood. Did you have good friends? Maybe early in your marriage and when the kids were young, it was all good.

When I asked the older folks in the nursing home who were going through hell about their past, many said that overall, they had pretty good lives. I know some had severe storms to go through, including the deaths of children and spouses, and they had cancer scares. But almost all people will say that their past was pretty good. They are thankful for the lives they had. That does not mean every period in their lives was good. However, they have a bigger picture of their lives as a whole. Looking back, they know that a few years of depression does not make for a bad life. Can we learn from them?

Have you had success in your life? Have you had any educational accomplishments, good jobs, successful projects, or hobbies? Did you raise healthy, happy kids, and provide for your family financially? These things may be gone now, but nothing can take away your memories. They happened. They were real. Be thankful for them. You can spend your time being sad about what is gone, or just be happy that you had them.

"Tis better to have loved and lost, than never to have loved at all."—Alfred Lord Tennyson

Have you had love in your life? Hold on to that, even if it is no longer. Do I miss my mother who died when I was young? Of course! But I am still thankful I had a great mom! I work with many widows and widowers. Some of these people dearly loved their spouses and miss them terribly. But I would rather be in their shoes and have had the love of my life who dies than to have never found love at all. I try to use this logic as one step in the process to help them appreciate the blessings in their lives.

When I first started working in nursing homes, one of the first guys I worked with and became close to, had a bad reaction to anesthesia from elective surgery and passed away suddenly. I went to the bathroom and cried! I did not like this nursing home stuff! Psychological patients are not supposed to die! It happens to medical doctors, sure, but not us. However, I quickly learned to love working in nursing homes.

Throughout the twenty years I've been working, I have had countless close relationships with people whom I have adored and loved. I have had to encounter multitudes of losses in the process. But I still treasure my job. Every person I've lost and missed was a person I had the pleasure of getting to know. There was some degree of affection and love there and that love made the pain worth it. So as I look back on my life as a whole, I'm thankful for the love I have had, despite all the losses and the hurt. Every loss equals the love that you had! Every love in your life is a jewel to be treasured!

Something happened a long time ago to be thankful for that can help keep things in perspective. Jesus died on the cross for you.

"But God showed his great love for us by sending Christ to die for us while we were still sinners" (Romans 5:8).

From a godly perspective, we all have *the* primary reason to be thankful. Many of us who were raised in Christian homes or go to church regularly hear this all the time. Unfortunately, it is repeated so often we can often take it for granted and not appreciate how amazing this fact is. You have the God who made every little and big thing. He is all-knowing and all-powerful; yet, He went to great lengths to show you His great love. He gave up the palaces of heaven to come down to a shack in the desert to live a miserable life and be tortured and killed to help you in the storm you are currently in and the big storms of life overall.

While this is a common fact in history for all of us, what has God done for you personally in your past? When did you come to accept Him and how did that happen? If you always remember believing, then you can be thankful you were lucky and cared for enough to be taught about Jesus from the start.

If you were not raised in a Christian family, or were not a believer early on, but came to believe in Jesus later, then what was the situation that led you to that decision? Several people must have shared with you and prayed for you, which led you to believe. Of course, God Himself played a big part in that. As we know, He actively pursues us and wants none to perish. Those are big things to be thankful for indeed!

Your Present
This is usually the hardest time to find positive things to be thankful for because you are probably currently in a storm. And it can be difficult to find things to be thankful for in the middle of a storm. All you can see is the rain and the lightning. It is so difficult to see anything else good, but you must look around and see what there is to still be thankful for. Remember that a depressed mind will look for all the bad things

in your life to be depressed about. However, you do not want to be depressed, do you? You want to feel better. So you must gather all the positive evidence you can, don't you?

When the storms are more difficult, and we are having trouble finding anything good to be thankful for, we may have to go to the basics of life. We still need to be thankful for the foundations of survival such as food, water, and shelter. But do not take those simple basic things for granted. When people are battling cancer, they and their loved ones are praying and fighting to have nothing more than to live. Here in America, most have more than enough to live and there are many programs and charities to help those who are struggling. The point is that our prosperity causes us to take these basics of life for granted that most of humankind throughout history did not.

Many around the world today do not have the basic necessities, especially once they are seriously impaired or elderly. Many of my elderly clients really do not have much to be thankful for currently. They have lost so much of their past life and loves, not to mention their freedom and dignity. I do have to point out that they have food, shelter, medical care, and at least some staff and me who truly care for them. Luckily, this older generation do know what it is like to go without, even the basics. The depression era generation is mostly gone now, but their children still remember what life was like in those days. Thus, try not to take your blessings for granted.

Again, you can still feel sad, but try to add some positive thoughts. They are true thoughts. Do you still have some people in your life? Most of us only have a handful of people with whom we are really close and can depend upon. We may have many more who genuinely care about us but are not as close and would be there more if they knew we needed them. Do not think because a set number of close people are not around you that your life is miserable. That is not a very rational *expectation* to have (as discussed in the last chapter). Also, do not take others' love for granted just because they have always been there. Family can often be like this.

Do not think that just because your dad has always been there that his love is not important or does not matter when your boyfriend has broken up with you. "Well, he is just my dad. He is supposed to love me. He has to, so it doesn't count." Do you still have some family members and friends who are always there for you? Do they adore and love you? Do they want nothing but the best for you, even if they have not been around as much as you would like? They may be in the midst of their own storms. They may be a little selfish and thoughtless, not realizing how much you need them, but that does not mean they do not care about you and love you.

Are you successful at something? Your life might be going terribly in one aspect, but are there still parts of it that are going well? Should you be proud of yourself for certain aspects of your life? Have you made a good living financially? Have you been a good parent? Do you have gifts and talents that can be used in the future? Focusing on these positive areas of life has been a great coping strategy for many people who are suffering. Some put their energy on their kids, jobs, or ministries after one area of their lives has fallen apart.

Do you have your health? Do not even take that for granted. Some people's storms are their health. I work with patients in the nursing home who are sad and depressed because their health is poor, amongst their other losses. And they have every right to be sad. But sometimes I try to get them to appreciate what they have before they lose it. I want them to see where they will probably be in a couple of years. They may not be able to even walk. That is even sadder, I know, but I want them to appreciate the abilities they still have before they lose them. You too can appreciate what you have because others do not have even that.

Your Future

We do not usually think of being thankful for the future. After all, the future has not happened yet, so how do you know what to be thankful for. Well, with faith in a God who knows our future, we can be thankful for many things.

For someone who is depressed, the future can often be the hardest place to find things to be thankful for. Part of what defines depression is a sense of hopelessness; thus, it is difficult to be thankful for a future you think will be worse than it already is! You assume that because things have been bad they will continue to be bad. Since you have been rejected in the past you will continue to be rejected. Since you have failed in the past you will continue to fail in the future. Since your loved ones are no longer with you, then your heart will always be empty and you will never be happy again. However, I have tried to make a case that you cannot trust your depressed, negative feelings when in a storm. Know that these hopeless thoughts are very narrowly focused. As we looked at previously, your mind only wants to see the negative. I know that looking at tomorrow can be terribly overwhelming, and I know I cannot make those negative worries just go away. But can you also look at the positives of tomorrow?

There is one simple, and undeniably true concept: past failures do not equal future failures. Just because you have rolled a seven on a pair of dice twice in a row does not mean it will come up again. Look at how many businessmen have succeeded greatly after numerous failures. Sam Walton of Walmart was just one typical example of having several failed businesses before he finally got it right. I did not find a good marriage initially, but I eventually ended up with love. Many older people can tell you countless stories about hard times in their lives that then turned out okay. Were these times hard for them? Yes! They will tell you that it hurt like hell. But life went on and there were more good times to come.

Faith – The Key to a Great View of the Future
You might think, "How can I be thankful for what hasn't happened yet?" The answer: faith.

"Faith is the substance of things hoped for, the evidence of things not seen" (Hebrews 11:1 NKJV).

For those of us who believe in Jesus Christ, the future really *should* be the easiest thing to examine to help you get through the storm. The task is to find things to be thankful for. Your future as a Christian *should* be the easiest source of the things to be thankful for. If we keep these things in our minds every day, it will help us immensely in our attitude toward our current problems. But this is not just blind faith in rainbows or a vague spiritual higher being. This is faith in God who knows you personally, has an intense deep love for you, and who is all-knowing and all-powerful. He tells us He will *"make all things work together for good to those who love God"* (Romans 8:28).

There are many good definitions of faith. I like the definition that faith is reasoned trust. None of us will put our trust in something unless it has earned it. When we sit in a chair, we have put our trust in that object to hold us up and not let us fall. We trust in the chair because, in the past, everything that looked like a chair held us up.

While there are many religious faiths out there, and some people will believe in any odd thing, most people would not put their religious faith in just anything. A religious belief, including atheism, should have a well thought out set of beliefs that have some historical basis and are logically consistent. A religious faith should have solid answers to the following questions about life: our origin, meaning of life, morality, and destiny. Christianity has solid answers to these questions.

We have a great book called the Bible that teaches us how faithful and reliable God is. There is a long history through thousands of years right up to the present-day Israel, in which God has, and is intervening. He is showing us He has a plan for rescuing us and is following through as He prophesied He would. We also have our own personal experiences with Jesus Himself. Most of us have gone through experiences where we can look back and see how He was there for us and turned bad situations into something good.

God has proven He knows and controls the future. In the Old Testament, God gave hundreds of prophecies of Jesus' first coming, and they all came true. Jesus then said He would die and come back to life. He did just that! This is all in addition to hundreds of stories about God's ability to be all-knowing and in control of our world. So when this guy says He will make a better world for us, I think we can trust He knows what He is talking about!

Heaven

We can certainly be thankful to God for what He will do for us in the near future in this world. God can help us miraculously in our current storms, or, at least, He promised to hold our hands and be there for us. But honestly, He did not promise us a great life in this world. He promised a great life in the next world. That is a promise we can bank all of our happiness on.

Chapter Takeaways

1. The "peace that passes all understanding" is achieved by staying thankful.
2. We can all be the spoiled little girl.
3. Categorize your blessings in three categories: past, present, and future.
4. Put your faith in a God who has proven Himself trustworthy. This will help you keep in mind the reality of how good your future is and how loved you are!

Chapter 9

Heaven: Our Eternal Hope

"Do not grieve as those who have no hope" (1 Thessalonians 4:13)

We discussed earlier that when we are depressed or experiencing terrible storms, we might secretly long for a magical fairy godmother or a knight in shining armor to come rescue us. Well, there actually is a knight who will come on His white stallion. His name is Jesus. He is not just here for us in the here and now. He will help us more than we could ever imagine in the future. Literally, all of our problems will be solved.

Yes, He very well might come right away when we call. Pray for your needs to be met today. He might help us by giving us what we need in dramatic ways. We know He is always there when we are depressed. He wants to hold and comfort us. It might come in some unexpected way, which works out better than we could have imagined. He might say "not yet." He might say "no." Jesus can also help us by kicking us in the butt and telling us to get over ourselves and to start caring for His glory and the welfare of others more than ours. It might be to just hold us and to let us cry until we are ready to gain the quiet strength to move on. One day, He will come literally and rescue us for good, but not right away or as fast as we want.

There is something even grander than what God can do for us on this earth—heaven. Jesus promised us many times to make things better for us in the next one. The whole point of Him descending to earth, dying for us, and coming back to life again, was to rescue us in our storms, to save us. He did this so we can live with Him in paradise forever.

We talked a great deal about changing what we can and accepting what we cannot. If you cannot change your situation and if you are stuck with your problem, and are struggling to accept it, there is one final solution for change and to give you enough drive to keep going. This storm you are currently in is not permanent! It may be long-lasting. It may hurt. You might be sad. I cannot take that away. But can I add a little hope that is guaranteed?

Let not your hearts be troubled. You believe in God; believe also in me. My Father's house has many mansions. If it were not so, I would have told you. I am going to prepare a place for you. And if I go and prepare a place for you, I will come again and receive you to myself; that where I am, there you may be also. (John 14:1-3 NIV)

Heaven is *not* a fairy tale. It is easy to think of it as an ideal, a metaphor, something far off in another world that does not really have anything to do with us in the real world. Many strong, faithful Christians only think of heaven as an abstract ideal. They may have a vague idea of it, but it is a concept, not a reality. Heaven is real, very real! It is our hope. The word "hope" in the Bible means a guaranteed promise. We use the word hope to mean a wish. "I hope dinner is good tonight. I hope I win the lottery." But the Bible uses the word to reassure us that Jesus will be there for us, guaranteed.

Fear of Death

In order for us to get excited about heaven, we first have to conquer our fear of death. The idea of heaven cannot motivate you if you are afraid to die. Faced with a life or death situation, would you panic and be afraid of dying? Sadly, many younger Christians have some fear of death, and by younger, I mean under the age of 60. A life or death situation can be a test of fire, revealing the true nature of our faith. If you were having a heart attack, being mugged, or your plane was going through terrible turbulence as you were landing, would you be terrified? It might be true that you have thought this through and are not at all afraid of dying, but there is fear.

A little fear in the first instance is normal due to our survival instincts. When you have your first heart attack, fear will most likely be your first natural response. But what if you had a few moments to think about it? Hawaii just went through a big scare. A mission warning alarm was sounded, with the threat from North Korea looming. I was listening to a sermon from a pastor on Youtube. He said his family gathered together and was almost giddy with excitement, thinking that their physical life was near the end. He admitted they were actually a little disappointed that nothing happened. This demonstrates a deep faith that knows where we are going.

I knew an elderly lady once who just could not take the pain anymore from her dialysis. Medically, if a person with renal failure stops dialysis, she will die in a week or two. Most do not consider this suicide, as it is just letting your body do what it is naturally trying to do. I had to talk to her first to make sure that she was not making a rash decision out of a temporary emotional state. I talked with her about this choice, and indeed she was making a rational and spiritual decision. I pointed out how brave it was to just walk head-on into death like that. She looked at me as if I was stupid.

She said, "What's so brave about going to be with your Maker?" Her simple, childlike trust and faith were beautiful. Honestly, I felt foolish afterward for even asking the question. We should all have such a simple idea of death. It is the truth; isn't it?

If we really believe there is a big God in the sky who made us, then we should have no problems jumping off the cliff and trusting that He will catch us. I used to play a game with my young daughter to teach trust. I would let her stand on the kitchen counter, facing backward, body stiff, and allow her to fall backward into my arms. At first, I would have my hands right there so she could feel me, then I would lower her upper body. But then each time I would move my hands further back until eventually, she would free-fall backward. She was brave and did so well. She did this only because she trusted that I was strong enough and loving enough to not let her fall and get hurt. Isn't our Father in heaven much stronger and more loving than we are?

The fear of death is something strongly ingrained in almost all cultures throughout mankind's history. Learned men and religious men have forever tried to find ways to cheat death, but always to no avail. Even those of us who were raised in a Christian culture, are still taught that death is the enemy. Doctors try desperately and at all costs to keep patients alive. I walk into my nursing homes and sometimes find out that one of my patients has passed suddenly. My instant, learned reaction is one of sadness, not for me, but for him. Then I start to think, depending upon the person, "Wait, no, this was a good thing." The person was hurting and had lost everything important to him. He believed in Christ and was longing to be in heaven with Him. This is a good thing.

A big problem is that we do not know what is on the other side. Many people deep down think they have faith there is life after death, but it is just an idea, a hope. Truly, no one has seen the other side for sure and come back with proof such as pictures. It is the fear of the unknown. It is a common, understandable, and practical defense mechanism. It would be nice to have brochures of heaven, showing the beauty that awaits us, with a big description of the wonderful joys and family time we will all have. But this is where faith comes into play. God has given a brochure; it is within the Bible.

Many of my elderly patients are not afraid of dying; they long for it. While very few are suicidal, many pray humbly, "God, if you can, take me now." The storm for them is not death; it is living in a bad state with no chance of getting better and yet too healthy to die anytime soon. Older Christians are often not afraid of dying. They have lost many people and faced numerous deaths. They have looked at their ages and accepted, begrudgingly, that death is truly going to hit them too at some point. Time and situations have forced them to accept in their hearts, not just their heads, that death and heaven are real. They have accepted what they cannot change. They use this to comfort themselves, knowing their problems will soon be solved. On the other hand, I do have several patients who want to die to get away from their current problems with no thought or joy in where they are going.

I have looked forward to death since I was sixteen after my mother died. I simply thought, "Hey, when I die, I get to be with my mother." When I started working with the elderly I studied heaven more and used the idea to encourage others. No. I am not trying to die any time soon. My family needs me. However, I am not at all afraid of death. I am certainly afraid of the pain of dying, and if it would be a long, slow, painful death, but not of death itself. Remember the setting I am usually working in—nursing homes.

A personal example of how the idea of heaven gets me through a storm is one involving being hurt by my daughter. I only have one biological daughter. She was the love of my life. For fifteen years we did everything together, just the two of us. We went to the zoo, movies, the park, the amusement parks, and the mall. I made her breakfast every single weekend and put her to bed reading books together every single night. However, I divorced her mother and she never forgave me. I was not innocent at all in the whole mess, and I am not here to argue who was right or wrong in all that. My point is that I lost the love of my favorite person in the world. Now, I am hoping that as she gets older, we can work things out and I will have her love and respect again. But it very likely will not happen. I grieved hard for years about this. I bawled my eyes out so many times. It was like the death of my child.

What got me through and helped put a smile on my face again, was this very concept that I am teaching. I *know* that one day she will be by my side again saying, "I love you, Daddy" (crying as I write this). This *will* happen in heaven. We will both see clearly and understand more in-depth. We will be so loved by God up there that we will not have any animosity or grudges. Amends will be made. We will all be reconciled with each other. Knowing this truth set me free and gave me hope.

The Magnificent Beauty of Heaven

Heaven is totally overrated. It seems boring with clouds and listening to people play the harp. It should be somewhere you can't wait to go, like a luxury hotel. Maybe blue skies and soft music were enough to keep people in line in the 17th century, but heaven has to step it up a bit. They're basically getting by because they only have to be better than Hell (Starbucks coffee cup).

This is an actual quote I found on a Starbucks cup one morning. It was part of a controversial campaign where they put different odd quotes on the cups to stir up debate. At first, I was appalled. But what is sadder is that this is a popular notion, even among many

Christians. People seriously think heaven is just sitting in the clouds singing and playing harps all day, every day—for eternity. Ugh! I don't think the hope of heaven would motivate me too much if this were the case. But this is not at all what the Bible teaches us heaven is like!

"What no eye has seen, what no ear has heard, and what no human mind has conceived, the things which God has prepared for those who love Him" (I Corinthians 2:9 NIV).

This is a much better verse to describe how amazing heaven is. Think about your best idea for a resort vacation. Maybe Hawaii or a chateau in the woods overlooking a mountain lake. Imagine five-star luxury, amazing food, and perfectly manicured landscapes. Picture gorgeous flower beds, green lush lawns, sparkling clear water, and beautiful, big full trees everywhere you look. There are bright, vibrant colors that you have never seen before. Imagine your health is better than ever with no more aches and pains. You have tons of energy, and you are never tired. And all of your favorite friends and family members are there, especially the ones you so dearly loved and who broke your heart when they passed. They are there with you too! But this does not even begin to describe what heaven is like. Like the above verse says, we cannot even begin to imagine how wonderful it will be. I encourage you to read good books about heaven and near-death experiences. Whenever I get too down, I listen to stories on Youtube and remind myself what is coming.

That is all some of my patients have left. They are crippled and in bed and can't do anything for themselves. There is no hope of them getting better physically. They're lonely, very lonely, as no one comes to visit them. They miss their spouses and everything else good that they've lost in this life. Realistically, these people have no hope of getting better on this earth. I cannot tell them to just

"Hang in there; it will get better." On this earth, it will not get better. This is why they need more than anything to know the real hope that there's something more than this life. I believe God wrote about heaven in the Bible to give us this hope.

"Set your minds on things above" (Colossians 3:2 NIV).
"In light of Heaven, the worst suffering on earth, a life full of the most atrocious tortures on earth, will seem to be no more serious than one night stay at an inconvenient hotel."—Mother Teresa

Mother Teresa immersed herself in the lives of the people she was serving. All she devoted her life to was helping people who were poor and sick. Yet, she knew that in the big scheme of things, suffering was only a small part of their existence. She knew that being up there, looking back, this world will not seem so bad. Mother Teresa was able to use this information to help herself and those around her keep their spirits up amid unbearable suffering.

To further comprehend this perspective, imagine you go on a vacation for two weeks in Europe. You travel all over and spend each night in a different city and you are having a great time. However, the hotel on one of those nights turns out to be terrible. The room is old and run down. It smells. The walls are thin. The bed is lumpy, and you get no sleep at all. But the rest of your trip goes well. Would you say you had a bad vacation overall? Truly, it would be more wonderful than the best vacation at the best five-star resort!

Two thousand years before Mother Teresa, the apostle Paul had this perspective as well. He too knew suffering. He suffered greatly. He had chronic pain, a thorn in his flesh that would not heal. We are not sure what he suffered from, but it seems obvious he was in pain. He received forty lashes five different times. He was shipwrecked, imprisoned repeatedly, and had no real family to love him.

"I consider that our present sufferings are not worth comparing with the glory that will be revealed in us" (Romans 8:18 NIV).

He once admitted he would rather leave this world, as many of us often feel. He said, *"I am torn between the two: I desire to depart and be with Christ which is better by far, but it is more necessary for you that I remain in the body"* (Philippians 1:23-24 NIV).

This verse helped pull me out of my own suicidal depression when I was sixteen years old after my mother passed away. Knowing that Paul, therefore, God also, understood my pain and longings helped validate my feelings. This, along with believing God had more of a purpose for me in this life gave me the strength to keep going.

I am like a kid before Christmas thinking about heaven. I get so excited about how wonderful it will be. We know we will be with our families. We know we will be strong and healthy. We know heaven will be a time of rest with nothing but peace and happiness. However, all those things do not compare to true joy. This joy *should* make our worst storms seem like light summer rain. The best thing about heaven is Jesus, the presence of God Almighty, and the Holy Spirit all around us. I do not think I can fully comprehend how beautiful this is going to be, how safe, secure, and loved we will feel in God's presence. I know this in my head cognitively, but I can only imagine how awesome it will feel.

Will You Get In?
How do you know you will go to heaven? I do not want to go into a long dissertation on theology or take the focus off the topic, but

I have to address this a little. First and foremost, the Christian perspective is,

- We are sinners and have turned our backs on God. *"For all have sinned and fallen short of the glory of God"* (Romans 3:23).
- God is perfect and holy; thus, He cannot be with us. We cannot make ourselves worthy on our own through good works.
- God sent His Son Jesus to die on the cross to pay for our sins. *"For God so loved the world that He gave His only begotten Son, that whoever believes in Him shall not perish but have everlasting life"* (John 3:16 NKJV).
- We must believe, accept Him as our Lord and ask forgiveness. There is no other way to get to heaven. *"No one comes to the Father except through me"* (John 14:6 NIV). If we could get to heaven any other way, this wouldn't have been necessary.

I know many are worried they have screwed up too much for God to forgive them. I ask most of my patients what they think will happen to them after they die. Ninety-five percent of my clientele have a Christian worldview, with about half being Catholic and half Protestant. Many of them are afraid they are not good enough to get into heaven. It is hard to get excited about going to heaven if you think you will be turned around by St. Peter at the gate. However, it is so easy to enter. The short answer is that you cannot be good enough, but Jesus was good enough for you.

The Bible is full of stories of people who did terrible things. But they repented and did great things for God, having been fully forgiven and loved by Him. God will forgive you for *anything* if you just come to Him.

"If we confess our sins, He is faithful and just and will forgive us our sins and purify us from all unrighteousness" (1 John 1:9).

Think about your love for your children. No matter what terrible things they do to you, if they sincerely come back and apologize, you forgive them and are so glad they came back to you. We are God's children who He dearly loves much more than we do our children. God is so good He wants to give us the great gift of heaven. But wait. There's more! He also wants to give us a bonus gift. (Hurry now! The first 50 callers will receive this bonus.) He wants to give us the additional gift of knowing now ahead of time, that we will definitely be going to heaven.

"I write these things to you that believe in the name of the Son of God, so that you may know that you have eternal life" (1 John 5:13).

This has been one of my favorite verses because of the small little phrase so "that you know." It does not say, "I write these things so that you can have eternal life." It says, "I write these things so that you will know that you have eternal life." He wants us to know *now*! He knows we are hurting. He knows we need some hope and encouragement to keep us going.

Advice from Your Future Self

So how can we use this view of the future in heaven to help us? We know that better times are coming, so hang in there. But the knowledge of the certainty of heaven and better times needs to be deeper than that. We can learn to really look at our lives right now from a different perspective. Up to this point, most of us have been looking at our lives only through this small little myopic lens of our current perspective. We tend to look at our lives as just consisting of today, the near-term future, and the past. The near-term future usually scares us, and the past shames or depresses us because the good ol' days are gone. But if you could see the bigger picture, the forest, instead of just the trees, your whole outlook today could change for the better. This is the truth of your existence. The whole forest is the truth. The trees are real, but if you think they are all that exist, then your view of truth is skewed.

To give a good demonstration of this perspective, let us use an example that most of us can relate to. Do you remember how you were sixteen-ish years old and a boyfriend/girlfriend broke up with you? It was a very real and sad time. You might have thought no one would ever love you again, that, in fact, you were not even lovable or capable of ever being loved by anyone. In these situations, severe depression can set in and some people even become suicidal.

Fast forward several years into the future. Numerous loves have come and gone. Successes have been experienced. Life was lived. Most people who are happily married had previously had their share of heartaches before they found "the one." The sadness and hopelessness of the mindset of that sixteen-year-old seem a little dramatic looking back on it now.

I remember in college, my high school/college girlfriend broke up with me after cheating on me with another guy. I was devastated and severely depressed. I am not even sure why I was so heart broken. I wasn't in love with her. I had tried breaking up with her just a few months before. Looking back, I think I was so depressed because of the blow to my ego. How dare someone who was not even good enough for me break up with *me*? Not that I thought I was all that at the time, though it was very stupidly arrogant nonetheless. I felt unlovable.

I finally got over it when I begrudgingly accepted I was not going to get my way and it was over. After I learned and grew up more, I became more and more ashamed of how badly I reacted to that event. It was really quite silly, though it seemed very serious at the time.

Imagine if my nineteen-year-old self was able to talk to my older self. What could I learn? Without knowing any details of what happened in my life, I would have had proof that there was so much more to come. Now, we know many of us are too egocentric and prideful at a young age to listen to our parents' advice. But a wise teenager/young adult would. As we get older, we realize that our parents often knew what they were talking about, and we kick ourselves because we did not listen. Some of our biggest storms could have been prevented, or, at the least, minimized, if we had listened to someone older and wiser who had been through life already.

What if we could talk to our future heavenly selves? No matter what age we are now, we are all still young, immature, and naive little kids compared to how we will be up in heaven.
"For now we see in a mirror dimly, but then face to face" (I Corinthians 13:12 NKJV).

While we do not know the details and depths of what is to come, we do know several things. We know we will be safe and secure, loved and healthy, surrounded by family and friends. Do we really need to know anything else? Can we be the wise children who listen to our elders? While we are still here in this life, we can often look back and laugh at ourselves for how dramatic we were as I did with my college breakup. Many of us have had times when we panicked or were upset about how things were going, only to see that things turned out for the best. We hated that we lost that job and were afraid we could not pay the bills. However, those seemingly bad events led us to better jobs or careers we would never have found.

Imagine what we will think when we are up there and in heaven looking back on our earthly lives. At that time, we will be at peace and have security knowing all will be good forever. We will have nothing to ever worry about again. What will we think about how we are handling our problems right now? I am sure we will laugh and shake our heads at how *if we had only realized how well it was going to be, we would not have become so darn upset and panicked.*

Therefore, if we had this richer, deeper faith, even the worst of problems here on the earth would seem like no big deal once we are up there. Keep in mind that we will understand things better than we do now. Our faith will be realized. There will be no guessing or hoping. All will be fully known. Ideally, we should have more of this faith now. However, can we use this logical head knowledge that we have of heaven to actually increase our faith today? Increasing this faith could then dramatically increase how we view and then cope with these issues. But we must be more purposeful in our thoughts. We must actively work to remind ourselves of these biblical truths to help them sink into our hearts.

So, let us put this to practical use. Your marriage has fallen apart. Divorce is looming or now final. You feel rejected and lost. As I have been saying, it is normal to be sad and devastated. I cannot take that away from you. You are grieving that loss and, by all normal human accounts, you should be sad. However, if you have truly thought about your faith in a loving God and the reality of future peace in heaven, then this is not really devastating. The divorce will still hurt like the dickens, but there is a guarantee of something more, something that has just enough strength to get you through each day. This something is the promise of a day when you will feel fully loved and will never be rejected again. Devastating is when it will be bad *forever*.

Let us look at an even more devastating storm. Pretend your only daughter, just fifteen years old, was killed in a car wreck. By any human standards, that is a tragic event, and no one would fault the parents for being depressed and truly overwhelmed with despair. However, the truth, the hardcore, undeniable truth, is that once they are in the security of heaven, they will again live side by side with that daughter. They will not be upset at all about the short delay after her death. All tragedies will be overcome by God's grace up in heaven. Nothing! The worst of human suffering will not compare to how amazing everything will turn out in the next world.

Interestingly, this premise is the topic of my next book. It will be a novel in which a woman is desperate, and God gives her wisdom by letting her face her future self who guides her into the truth of God's love.

Well, He's in a Better Place

The knowledge of the truth of heaven can significantly help with anxiety and grief. The death of a loved one is one of the major causes of our storms. Losing a loved one is devastating. We get sad and depressed and often want to give up. Most of us have lost someone significant who we think died too soon. Just about everyone ends up losing someone eventually. It sucks, and there is no way around it, even with the best faith and mental health. Even Jesus wept.

However, death is not the end. If you believe in Christ, you believe in the Bible and you have to change your perspective from what the world teaches us. There is a supernatural world. God exists, right? He is capable of doing amazing, supernatural things, right?

Jesus died and came back to life, right? Do you believe God is powerful or not? Do you believe what He said or not? Is He trustworthy or not?

If you believe this, then it is a fact that His words are true and heaven is real. Thus, death is nothing more than going from one location to another, to a much better location. I know it is hard to see because there are no brochures to look at and no Youtube videos showing travel vloggers on their trip to heaven. Wouldn't it be nice to have pictures and videos of heaven? But God wants us to trust Him. That is a big part of what this world is all about, learning how to trust God, our Creator and that He knows what is best for us.

So when we say, "Well, at least he is in a better place." We should mean it. He is—if he has asked Jesus to forgive him. He is partying and having a grand time. Feel sorry for yourself that you have to be without him, for a bit anyway. But be happy for him! It is okay to feel both happy and very sad.

Imagine losing your three young daughters and beautiful wife in a car wreck. This is the true story of one of my elderly clients many years ago. Even in that awful situation, that man ended up living wonderfully with his whole family in paradise, and for many more years (forever) than those years that he was without them here in this world.

"Hey, honey, remember that time back on Earth when you had to be without the kids and me?"
"Ohhh, yeah. I forgot about that. Ehhh. What do you want to do today?"

That situation is the truth. Nothing is catastrophic for a Christian.

We can know we will be with family in heaven in the future. First, it is the nature of God. He values our relationships with each other dearly. God would not change and throw away our relationships in heaven. But I also love that Scripture points to being with family in heaven. Take Judges 2:10: "After that whole generation had been gathered to their ancestors." This is just a nice way of saying, "after they died." However, by saying it this way, notice that it points out, as a matter of fact, that they were with their families after they left this earth. This is very important and should give us hope.

"O death, where is your sting? O grave where is your victory?" (1 Corinthians 15:55).

Reconciliation

A major contributing aspect of the hope heaven brings is the promise that we will be reconciled to each other one day. Our problems in our relationships are responsible for many of the storms in our lives. Can it help you to get through this life, knowing there will be no discord in heaven? As long as you and the people in your life have faith in Jesus, all will be well.

We want life to be fair. When storms hit us, we often act as if someone has done us wrong. Honestly, we may want revenge or restitution. We certainly want justice. Or maybe, humbly, all we want is resolution and reconciliation. We must know that things will be resolved. There will be harmony. The hurt people have caused you will all be worked out.

Of course, none of us are innocent. Some of us have caused our own storms with our selfish or foolish actions and are wallowing in shame and self-pity. We are afraid of facing certain people in heaven. But they will forgive us.

I am well aware of the many big sins I have committed to hurt people, some of which were very severe. However, I am also sure that I have hurt many people in ways I was never aware of. I want to know who I hurt and make amends, if at all possible. I at least want to validate their feelings and acknowledge what I did wrong. After all, that is all I want from those who have hurt me.

In our future heavenly home, we will be able to see and understand the wrongs we have committed. Our eyes will be open, and we will see completely and empathically from their perspective. We will be able to handle this guilt emotionally because we will have the security of knowing we will not be rejected by the person we had the conflict with or by God Almighty.

Confrontations and resolutions are stressful. However, it will be much easier and nicer up there. The beauty of this is knowing it will be all worked out and a deeper more meaningful relationship will grow.

I like the concept of *The Five People You Meet in Heaven*, by Mitch Albom. The primary character, Eddie, passes away and has to face several people whom he encountered during his life. Some helped him, and some suffered because of him. Eddie needs to reconcile with each of these and learn from them. The Bible strongly encourages us to reconcile with each other before going to God in worship here on this earth (Matthew 5:24). However, the Bible in no way says that we must reconcile with each other in the afterlife before we are allowed to move on. But we do know we will all be in harmony up there.

So how will it work there? Once we are in heaven, will we just instantly be at peace and love each other? Maybe we will be so darn happy, we will see things much more clearly. Will we be so unselfish and loving that we will let bygones be bygones and simply hug it out so to speak? Or maybe we will need to go through a process to learn more about our past experiences, what we did to hurt others and what effects it all had. We will have a greater capacity to understand the other person's perspective without all the baggage and defensiveness that keeps us from resolving issues here on the earth. In addition, we will also have a deep love for others and want to understand and make amends. Who knows? Maybe I will still have a job as a counselor helping people understand and reconcile. But one thing is sure—reconciliation *will* happen!

"In light of heaven, the worst suffering on earth will be seen to be no more serious than one night in an inconvenient hotel."—Mother Teresa

I love this quote from Mother Teresa. Here is a woman who knew all about severe suffering. All she devoted her life to was helping hurting people. Yet, she knew in the big scheme of things that suffering was only a small part of our existence. Can we remember this ourselves?

Chapter Takeaways

1. Heaven is real and the truth of our future.
2. Defeat your fear of death.
3. Heaven is beautiful and exciting. It will not be boring, floating on a cloud and playing a harp all day.
4. **Make sure you get in by believing in Jesus Christ who died on the cross for your sins.**
5. Today, think about what you will know about coping once you are up there.
6. Let this knowledge help with grieving the loss of loved ones.

7. Know that we will be reconciled with those Christians we have had trouble with.

Chapter 10

How to Make Sense of Suffering

"How could there be a good loving God with so much suffering in the world?"

Those who endure tough storms in life and feel alone and abandoned by God, often ask this question. It is also one of the main reasons why people do not believe in God. Admittedly, it is a big question. For me to help you cope with your suffering, you need to understand God's role in it. It is extremely important to delve into this subject to have a better understanding of our lives and God Himself. We want to have some knowledge of why things might have happened as they did. Knowing why can give us a sense of control, more trust in God, and ultimately some hope.

God is all-powerful and all-knowing. However, bad things happen. Therefore, God must be responsible. Simple logic, right? Not quite. Did you realize this argument comes with certain assumptions? First, do not assume because God is all-powerful that He causes everything to happen Himself. Yes, He could have created the world so He would orchestrate every little detail. But He did not. He did not want to. He did not want to because of love.

Many believers naturally assume that we are just actors in God's grand play. Something bad happens and we say, "Well, I guess that was just the will of God." My mother died at the age of 47 after having a stroke when I was sixteen. God must have caused it and wanted her to die, right? But as a good Christian, should I just accept that as God's will? Some people ask, "How can I be happy when God has made my life so miserable?" The question implies causality.

No, I do not believe God causes these bad things to happen. I also do not believe He coldly sits back and indifferently allows bad things to happen to innocent people. Indeed, I believe God is very sad about watching bad things happen to us. He *can* direct details in our lives. This does not mean He *is* necessarily directing every single detail. He *can*, but He does not.

Freewill and Love

The simple answer to why bad things happen to good people is it's because of human free will. It is not because of God. We are all free to choose our own paths. God does not force us. He gives us all choices and He does not *make* us do anything. He certainly does not make us do the right thing. All of our problems and every single bit of suffering originate from mankind doing our own thing. These actions are against God's desires and are root problems that end up hurting others and ourselves.

Why did God set up this whole world as He did with this concept of free will? Surely, He knew that with this freedom, we would mess it up big time and cause such terrible pain to human nature. Why did He do this? Did He not care about us or the consequences of our actions? Did He have some other grand purpose, maybe for His pleasure somehow?

Why does God allow suffering? Love. God wanted us to love Him, to truly love Him. Why does He want us to love Him? Because He first loved us. You cannot force someone to love you. It is only love if the person extending it has the free will to love.

To understand this better, let us pretend I was single and lonely and decided to make a robotic woman to give me the love I wanted. I could make her very pretty with great intelligence, personality, and charm. I could program her to love me. But would it be love? She would have no choice but to love me. I could program her to do this very well for me. But that is not love. What if I kidnapped a woman and put a gun to her head and forced her to love me? Again, no, that's not love.

My real-life wife chooses to love me, and she could choose to leave at any time. That is what makes it true love. She has free will and she chooses to stay with me. Some days, in the heat of the moment, I may give her reasons not to love me, but she chooses to keep loving me anyway.

It is the same with God. He wants us to love Him and freely choose to love Him. It would not be the same if He made us love Him. If He coerced us to love Him, if we were puppets or robots, then it would not be love. Therefore, we have the freedom to reject Him. Unfortunately, most people around the world do reject Him.

Those of us who are believers may choose to love Jesus, but this does not mean we choose to truly love Him, make Him our Lord, and do the right thing in our everyday decisions. Being Christians in no way makes us perfect. Far from it. This decision to believe in God *should* make us much better people, but that is often not the case either. We still have free choice and often choose to do our own thing and not what we know God would want us to do.

Unfortunately, the consequence of all this freedom means we make poor choices many times, and bad things happen as a result. Maybe the storms in our lives were caused by our own mistakes. Or perhaps they were caused by others' selfish, abusive, or careless mistakes. Indeed, all of creation was messed up by man's sin and choosing their way instead of God's way. Even natural disasters are caused by man not loving God. The Bible tells us how Adam and Eve's sin caused creation to groan (Romans 8:22). Maybe nobody knows what caused the storm in your life. But one thing is sure, all problems started one way or another because of mankind's decision not to love God, but rather, to do it their way.

If God stopped us from messing up and hurting each other, if He took away suffering, then He would be taking away our free will, our right to choose, and our independence. We cannot have a world free of suffering and, at the same time, have our free will and the freedom that comes with it. Would you want to live in a perfect world where we are all thoughtless, mindless robots? Or would you like to live in a world that has suffering but also real genuine love and freedom? We cannot have it both ways.

My Miracle of Understanding the Will of God from My Mother

I was sixteen. My mother came upstairs to give me a book *Understanding the Will of God,* by Leslie Weatherhead. Being a typical teenager, I just said thanks and tossed it aside for later. She had a stroke the next morning and died.

I picked this book back up a week or two later and began to read it. It hit me like a ton of bricks. Why did she give it to me the night before? Nobody knows ahead of time you will have a stroke. Yet, for some reason, she gave it to me at that time and it helped me to understand God's involvement in this world from a bigger perspective. It helped me to understand suffering, free will, and why bad things happen.

I do not know why my mother died. I don't know why my dad left. I do not know why my wife could not love me. I do know I hurt people. It was me, my selfishness, and my sin that caused their storms. However, whatever storm I found myself in, God had a preferred plan for me at that moment in my life. If you look to God, He will make something good come out of it, no matter how it started.

When my mother died, I became much closer to God because of it. Little did I know at the time that dealing with her two strokes and death would help me to grow closer to Him. Growing closer to God will reap the biggest reward and help you to have an immensely better life because of it. My mother's death and reading that book helped me to cope. But an even bigger thing came out of it. This experience helped to train me for a long career of assisting others to deal with similar storms. God used it all for good. God used that one book to help me and so many others. He knew she was going to go. He didn't stop it, but He worked through it, for good (Romans 8:28).

To put it simply, the book categorized God's will into three parts. In the grand scheme of things, God's will can be viewed in three ways: God's ideal will, God's circumstantial will, and God's ultimate will.

God's *ideal will* is what He wants us to do originally, in an ideal sense. He wanted us to follow and trust Him fully. However, He also gave us free will and we chose not to follow Him. We did our own thing. Sin and all the bad in the world were formed. So we find ourselves in storms of life and it's either our fault or someone else's.

So what does God want us to do given the circumstance we find ourselves in? This is His *circumstantial will*? God is the King of turning lemons into lemonade. He may not have put you in the storm you are in, but He can certainly make something good come out of it if you only look to Him and let Him.

That book Mom gave me described God's *ultimate will*. Sometimes God will do what He wants to do, regardless. Sometimes He will direct big things and little things for His glory. I fully believe we will get to heaven and learn about all the things God did to help us along the way, despite our sins. Miracles will happen all around us without us even knowing we were in danger. We will realize some of the bad things that happened to us were designed by God to help us avoid bigger problems or give us bigger rewards.

You might have begged God not to let your boyfriend break your heart. However, you would not have learned to be your own person and trust in God in a deeper way if He did not allow your boyfriend to harden his heart and leave you. You might have stayed in a miserable relationship forever if God hadn't stepped in. God is God. His ways are much higher than ours (Isaiah 55:8-9). We must trust Him, even if we do not understand. He has earned that trust. He has earned our faith.

God Is Not the Villain, He Is the Hero
We established that God did not cause the problem. To allow real love, God had to give us freedom and independence. This freedom, our refusal to follow our Creator's advice, has caused all of our problems. God is innocent. God is long-suffering, trying to get us to come back to Him (2 Peter 3:9). He is deeply saddened by our suffering.

So must a good, loving God take away our suffering without taking away our independence? He did the most loving thing He could do. He sacrificed His only Son to give us a chance to escape all the suffering. He paved the way to get us to heaven where there will be no more tears.

My Personal Vision of my Future
I woke up with a very vivid image in my head. I was looking down on myself. I was in a wheelchair, beside someone's bed, ministering to him.

God showed me in a dream once when I was about fifteen years old that I was going to be ministering to people in the future, but oh, yeah, small detail. I would be in a wheelchair myself. At the time, I did not know if it was a dream or a true vision and message from God. I was a healthy athlete (though not a great one). If this was a vision from God, then that meant I would not be able to walk! I was not at all happy about being crippled. However, I grudgingly submitted to God's will, if that was what He wanted.

Long story short, I went to college for ten years to become a psychologist and forgot about that vision. I had been working in nursing homes for about eight years when I remembered it again. And then it hit me. When I was working with my clients, there was often nowhere to sit. They would be in their beds and there were no chairs for me to sit in. So, where would I sit? In their wheelchairs! Several hours each day would be spent in a wheelchair. I tried to bring up God whenever I could, and thus, I considered myself a minister. I was ministering to people while in a wheelchair. I never lost my ability to walk at all. God never told me I would be crippled. I just assumed I would be.

The point is, God knew my career way ahead of time. He directed me on my path. I never had the idea of working in nursing homes. But I found myself doing this, and it has been the ideal job for me. God knew it. He showed me it ahead of time. He trained me for it, and He placed me in it. I am a big believer in free will. Yet, I can see how God has directed my path all the way. Even in my current big sets of storms, I believe there is a big purpose. Again, I am not sure God has caused these storms for a purpose. But if He did not cause them, He will indeed use them for His glory and someone's welfare. I would not have been pushed to write this book, which I pray will help you, if I hadn't gone through these storms. God works all things together for our good (Romans 8:28), but only if we love Him and follow His ways.

God is not to blame for our problems. In fact, it breaks His heart to see us suffer so much. He loves us and wants us to be happy. Completely opposite of God being to blame for problems is the fact that he has done everything to fix this mess! He gave us instructions on how to take care of each other and love each other. But we were too selfish and stubborn to benefit. We still are! So what did He do instead? He took the bull by the horns, and He made it happen so that we can have better lives here on the earth, yes, but especially in the next life. He did all the hard work. All we must do is believe Him and trust Him.

Chapter Takeaways
1. Bad things happen to good people because of freewill and our sins.
2. God gives us freewill in order to have true love and fellowship with us.

3. God deeply respects our independence.
4. God is never the villain. He is the Savior, despite our messes.
5. God can make lemonade out of lemons, but only if you look to Him and His will.

Chapter 11

The Meaning of Life and Our Purpose

"He has no design upon us, but to make us happy...Who should be cheerful, if not the people of God."—Thomas Watson

Instead of subtracting, maybe you should try adding. We have talked a great deal about getting rid of negative thoughts. This will always be true. However, you still have to add some positive thoughts. The negative facts about your struggles may be true, but so are the positives. I am not trying to minimize the degree of trauma brought on by your negatives, but I want to add in some positives. The negatives may be true, but so are the positives. This positive point I want to make is not just true, but profoundly true.

Throughout this book, I have tried to get you to look outside of yourself to not be too egocentric. The more egocentric you are the more depressed you get, and the more you distance yourself from others. Now, let us extend this further to a much deeper point. Try taking your eyes off yourself and your own problems. Put them on something else. Just about anything else would help. But how about putting them on the best thing—God.

For a Christian, this is an obvious answer, "Let go and let God." I will not deny that this is wonderful advice. However, it is also an overused cliche that has lost its full meaning for some. It cannot be dismissed as a primary truth just because it is a cliche. It became a cliche for a good reason, after all. We should learn to give up control and let God be in charge, even if it means we do not get what we want.

There is a lot more to my psychological advice here than just a simple cliche. Another cliché, "Just give it to God," never really meant much to me. It always sounded like a good idealistic goal, but not very practical. How do I give my stress and worries to God? I would pray for Him to help me let go of my stress, sure, but it was still there in my lap. Helping my patients cope with their storms and writing this book have forced me to contemplate how to put this ideal into practice. We must discover more deeply the wisdom that is in the whole idea of focusing on God to *let go*. I will talk about how pride and releasing control can help with this in the last chapter of this book, but for now, let us focus on another way of letting go.

What Is the Meaning of Life?

That is a big philosophical question; isn't it? Similarly worded questions about life: why are we here? Why were we made, and for what purpose? I think the answers to these questions should play a huge part in our search for how to cope with the storms of life.

God is our Creator. He made us. He is our inventor. He programmed the computer code that is our DNA. He is our Maker, Father, Friend, and Savior. Despite being able to design the galaxies of deep space, He still knows every hair on each of our heads and knew us before we were born. But why? Why did He create us? He had to have a reason.

Why would an all-powerful God bother to make such animals? Animals that can think deeply, love deeply, yet, all the while, seek their own pleasure to the extent that they hurt each other so much. They constantly turn their backs on the One who made them. God does not need us. He chooses to give us life and continues to pursue and love us. But why? For what purpose?

His purpose for making us was certainly not to just sit up there and do whatever we want Him to do for us. He did not make us just so that *He* could serve *us*. God is not a genie in the sky here to make our wishes come true. That would make us God and Him our servants. He alone is God and He alone is worth being served. I know I certainly am not God. And no one out there can do God-type things. Can anyone figure out how to make a tree out of nothing? (Job Chapter 38).

Why did God make us? He did not have to. He did not need anything. He is sufficient in and of Himself. God made us because He wants fellowship with us. He does not need it; He wants it. He wants a relationship with us purely out of love for us. That is all. He is the complete and ultimate epitome of love, to the extent that we cannot fathom.

This is the reason He made us: love! This is the first part of the meaning of life: God created us for a loving relationship with Him. Do not forget this fact. Never forget it, even in your darkest moments. I have said over and over that I do not want to minimize your negative thoughts. They are real and your life is hard. However, I want to add the other true thoughts, the positive ones. This is as positive as it gets people!

God made us to be with Him. But then we went and blew it. Yet, God's love continued to an even greater extent. God asked one thing of us in exchange for making us—one thing—to trust Him. He wants us to believe He knows what is best for us and then do as He says. But we all collectively and individually have said to God, "Nope, we got this God. We want to do it our way." Yet, He loved us enough to pursue us, even to the point of sending His only Son to save us.

"But God demonstrates His own love for us in this: While we were still sinners, Christ died for us"—*(*Romans 5:8).

He did not wait until we made ourselves pure and perfect. The primary difference between Christianity and every other religion in the world is that every religion attempts to make us better and good enough for God. Christianity states that we cannot make ourselves good enough. God is indeed the One who had to do the work to save us and bring us to Him. Unfortunately many, including Christians, believe falsely that we must follow certain rules to win our way to God. But no, God did all the work, and only God gets the credit and all the glory.

The second part of the meaning of life is our purpose. God made us to love and worship Him. When we look at the truly awesome love of God, in addition to His power and amazing works, we realize He is totally deserving of complete reverence and honor. He not only made us with the consciousness and ability to love, but He also saved us from ourselves in the most incredible way. His was the most remarkable act of love you could imagine. He lived a perfect life in this world and willingly gave it up. He was beaten and killed to help us be happy.

God has done great things in addition to His sacrifice. He created the amazing human body, all the plants, animals, and the perfect ecosystem we live in. He designed chemistry and physics. He set the stars in the sky throughout the entire universe. Each of these accomplishments could be studied in detail, each one revealing truly amazing pieces of engineering genius and evidence of a highly intelligent and personable God. In addition, God has the power to create anything out of nothing and to defeat any adversary easily, especially since He made everything. God deserves our worship!

Worship is our purpose. We were made to sit at God's feet. This is where we should be when we truly realize the truth of how God Almighty gave everything He could to save us. This is the most important point of our existence! He has given us everything, though we do not deserve it. He gave it purely out of ultimate, fierce love. We *should* be at God's feet, thanking Him and giving Him all of our accolades. This is what He deserves. This is what is right. **This is why we were made! We were made to worship Him.**

An amazing thing is the nature of this relationship. He could have easily just demanded us to serve him like slaves. He has earned this right. He could if He wanted to and would be morally able to do so. However, He takes this relationship to an even more personal, sweet, wonderful level giving us so much more than we deserve. God sees us as a friend (John 15:15). He calls us by the most affectionate terms. We are His beloved (Romans 9:25), His children (Galatians 3:26).

We are specifically children loved by the most wonderful, caring, giving Father you could imagine. We can call Him Abba Father, which literally means, Daddy, an affectionate term. Not only are we seen by God as His children, but as the firstborn, His dear children. In addition, He is the King of kings. Thus, we are not just children, but princes or princesses.

Why is worship so wonderful for our quest for emotional coping with the storms of life? It is because we are where we belong. When we put ourselves in our proper place at God's feet, we are whole and complete, on a deep spiritual level. It is what we were made for. We are a certain shaped block and the correct shaped hole for us is kneeling at the feet of God. There, things feel right; we sense that life is as it should be. When we are there, He is best able to take care of us, like the wonderful Dad He is. He can take care of His children, providing good things for us and protecting us.

When we are worshiping, even for a few moments, we feel happier as a result. It's the irony of happiness again. The more we take the attention off of ourselves and our happiness, and place it on

God, the happier we get. When we are in the place we were made for, all is right in our world.

"God does not exist to make a big deal out of us. We exist to make a big deal out of Him. It's not about you. It's not about me. It's all about Him."—Max Lucado, *It's Not About Me*

I have had the pleasure of having Max Lucado as my pastor for many years here in San Antonio. He has taught me a great deal about the messages in this chapter. We know we should be praying often. And when we are in a big storm of life, we tend to pray more than usual. Sometimes our prayer is simply, "Oh, God, please help me!" Or sometimes, it is simply, "Jesus!" Nothing is wrong with those prayers. There is power in the name of Jesus. But to get to the right place where we belong, we must pray in the right way. We all know we should pray and pray often, ideally, not just when we are hurting. If we spend time in prayer, humbly asking God what we should do in our lives every day, and taking the time to listen to Him, some of our storms could be prevented.

There are several elements to prayer:

- Asking God for help for ourselves
- Asking God for help for others
- Thanking Him for what is good in our lives

These are all good things to talk to God about, but the most important part is missing—praising and worshiping Him. We often get this mixed up with thanking Him. We only praise Him when something good has happened in our lives.

But can we tell Him how awesome He is even if our lives stink at the moment?

A common mistake we make is only praising God when we *feel* like it, when we are happy with how things have turned out, and we think He has blessed us. However, how often do we think about how great He is when things have not gone our way, or when things have been consistent, normal, or boring? Isn't He still great? Doesn't He still deserve our praise? Should we still be in our place at His feet, whether our lot in life is good or bad?

God Almighty is the same yesterday, today, and tomorrow. He is always good, always fair, always strong, and always loving. He is wonderful, even if you do not see Him doing something good for you. Do not get His actions mixed up with His character. He is always amazing, even when you do not see him doing amazing things. Did you figure out how to make a tree from nothing? Have you discovered how to build a machine as amazingly complex as a human with all its interconnected organs? In the book of Job, God gave Job an earful about the wonderful things He did, that no created being could ever do. Job learned to be humble and accept that only God is God.

Let us look at it selfishly for a moment. If we remain self-focused and do not make God our focal point, we will miss out on the opportunity to be happier. Our loss. We have the chance to feel more at peace, even in the midst of the storm, by going to the proper place we know logically we should be. God wants to give us those gifts of peace, which now, and ultimately, are much more valuable than simple material happiness in this world.

A vacation would be wonderful right now. I bet. Even a little trip to a day spa, maybe. Just the thought of getting away from your problems for a little while can help your stress. Think about prayer as a trip to the day spa. Sitting at God's feet, letting go of your problems, and just adoring Him, can take away your thoughts about your problems and the negativity. We give ourselves and our praise to Him, and we receive a great gift as a by-product. We feel better. Our problems seem smaller. We find peace and rest, even if for just a bit. Too bad we are such fleeting, easily distracted creatures and cannot stay in this good place emotionally all the time. Truth is we can, if we choose to stay focused on God's holiness.

Music can play a great role in this. Praise music is a fundamental staple for many people to keep them going through bad storms. I suggest getting together a playlist of good contemporary Christian songs or hymns, whichever you prefer. There are also many good modern versions of some of the best classic hymns. However, do not just use any good song. Create a playlist that only has songs about praising God. God will always be involved in any Christian song. But what is the primary subject of the song? Many gospel songs are about us, encouraging us to be better. No problem with these songs at all, but they are different from the ones that focus primarily on God. I have been using my primary go-to playlist for many years and through many storms. I cannot count the number of hours I have listened to these songs.

They do not become old to me either. I just think about the words and the meanings, and I go into my happy place— at His feet. I have included my playlist at the back of this book.

Casting Crowns' *Praise You in the Storm,* has been the fundamental inspiration for my entire ministry, Peace in the Storm, and this book. The lyrics, "You are who You are, no matter where I am," stick with me all the time. It is a bedrock of strength, no matter how hard the winds of the storm are hitting me and how scary it is. I know my foundation in Him will not falter.

Thus, if He deserves it and if we benefit from it, then we should do it. Praise Him. We should do this whether we feel like it or not. I have made the point many times in this book that you should do what you *know* you should do and not necessarily what you *feel* like doing. Cognitively tell God how wonderful He is for all that He has done, and who He is. The great thing is if we do this, we start to feel it. This is a great point in life. Act on what you know to be true, not on how you feel. Fake it until you make it. There is truth in that. Give God what He deserves, and you will reap the rewards for being with Him.

Chapter Takeaways

1. The meaning of life can be found in why God made us and for what purpose.
2. God made us for fellowship with Him and to worship Him.
3. When we worship God, we are in our natural right place in the universe.

4. We feel better emotionally when we quit looking at ourselves and our problems and just look at God.
5. Praise God in your prayer life and in song.

Chapter 12

Your Life Is More Than Fair

"For the wages of sin is death. But the free gift of God is eternal life in Christ Jesus our Lord" (Romans 6:23).

Do You Want Things to Be Fair?
When storms hit, it is easy to feel life has been unfair. You do your best and sometimes bad things just keep coming. You are a normal, decent person who is just trying to do what's right. You do not believe your loved ones or you deserve such bad experiences. You did not deserve to get fired. You did not deserve a cheating spouse. You did not deserve to have your daughter die in a car wreck. You did not deserve cancer. Sure, you are not perfect, and some storms may have been purely your fault, but you do not think you deserve this tragedy.

Perhaps you need to change your perspective, look at your thoughts, and evaluate them to see if they are helping you or bringing you down. Life may have been very unfair to you. What you wanted may not have been asking for too much. These thoughts of despair may not be irrational; however, are they helpful?

How do you automatically expect life to be decent? I ask again, are your expectations realistic? Nobody should expect any specific or repeated storms. However, this is life on this earth we are talking about. Maybe it is more rational to believe that this world *should* be unfair. As the older, wiser generation would often say, "Life ain't supposed to be fair."

We have to remember this world is not as it was meant to be. It is a sinful, fallen world. Adam and Eve's sin messed up the perfect world God prepared for us and since then every one of us has contributed. We are all sinners (Romans 3:23). Since some people never follow God's will, and all of us mess up on His will at times, problems in this world will happen—often. We only have ourselves to blame, really. So, then why expect good? Harsh, I know. But biblically, it is true.

Truth: Your Life Is Better Than Fair

Given the state of the world humans have produced, what is God's perspective of what is fair? After all, it is truly the one true perspective. It is the truth, the *real* perspective, not our own view of reality, but reality. I have not forgotten that this is ultimately about helping you cope with your storm and find peace. However, to get you to that point, we must see and understand that truth. We should always want to understand the full truth of any situation. "The truth will set you free" (John 8:32). We would be foolish to ignore a point of view that could help us, even if it is not pleasant to hear. Once we understand this, it is very good news.

The truth is, life is better than fair, no matter what horrific storms we go through. We are getting a better deal than we *should*. When it comes down to it, we should be extremely happy, compared to how bad things *should* be. I have tried to point out the end game of how great heaven will be. The objective of that chapter was to give hope. But we must also look at what the alternative to heaven could be, indeed, *should* be for us.

God made us to have a loving relationship with Him. But He is perfect and holy. He wanted us to love Him, but He wanted us to do so willingly. Thus, He gave us free will. With this free choice, we have chosen to live our way, not His way. He is perfect, and we are not. So He cannot let us be with Him in our impure condition, or else that would make Him impure, which is impossible.
God cannot be *anything other than* God.

Imagine a big white cloth, one that is pure, bright white. It has not a spot or blemish on it. Now, take a white strip of cloth with red spots on it. Try and sew it together with the pure white one. You cannot say the big cloth is pure anymore, can you? God is pure white. This is indeed what holy means. If He let us be with Him, while we are in our sins, then He would not be pure; He would not be holy. That just cannot be. God *must* stay pure and holy.

God is the author of all good. Anything apart from Him is not good or pleasant. We are the impure strips of cloth. We do not deserve to be with Him because, well frankly, we do not want to be with Him. Sure, we say we do, but do we? We want the benefits of His protection, love, and gifts, but we do not want to do things His way. We do not want to trust Him when we do not understand why? Imagine a child who wants all the protection, love, and material things a parent gives, but rebels all the time against the parents' rules.

Why *should* God give us all of the benefits of His power if we are constantly doing things our own way? Maybe you specifically are a generally good person for the most part, but you are not perfect. None of us are. It is not so much that we commit sin, as it is that we are sinners. The inner core of us wants to do it our way, not His. Faith could be defined as "a reasoned trust." We have good reason to trust God. He has proven His love and power. We *should* trust that He knows what is best for us. Obviously, we do not have much faith. Thus, we do not truly trust that God knows best.

God is all-loving. This is true. But He also has to be completely just and fair. People want to say that if God is such a loving God, why doesn't He let everyone into heaven? He will not do this. No, He cannot do this because to be perfect and holy, He has to be just and fair. Any good father cannot let his children go wild and reward them for doing whatever they want. Any good father wants to give his children gifts, but not if they are brats. A good father *cannot* turn his back on rebellion and distrust of him.

Imagine a judge has a son who is convicted of a crime in his courtroom. He loves his son, but he is guilty. Since he loves him so much, he wants to let him off the hook but is legally bound to uphold the law. So, he does the most loving thing he could do. He takes off his robe and serves his son's sentence for him. This is what God did by sending His only Son, Jesus, to die for us, for you. God has to be just, but He does all He can to get us back to Him. God did not cause the problem, but He did all He could to fix it.

What We Truly Deserve

What is fair? What would be a fair and just natural consequence of how we live our lives? We are not entitled to anything good just because we exist. Yes, God is a good, loving God, and He wants to give us good things. He has done all He can to give us wonderful, amazing things. But He does not *owe* it to us just because we exist. God is not our Master who is there just to please us. So, what do we deserve? The hard truth: hell. We deserve hell. *"The wages of sin is death"* (Romans 6:23). We deserve nothing good in our lives. I know that sounds harsh.

Many people may feel they are already in hell here on the earth. This world is not easy at all. However, hell is much, much worse. In hell, there is nothing good. God is the author of all good. No God, no good. Hell is just the absence of God, the absence of good.

"For Christians this present life is the closest they will come to Hell. For unbelievers, it is the closest they will come to Heaven."—Randy Alcorn

People like their independence. They do not like to be told what to do. Working in nursing homes, I can tell you for certain that this is a major psychological issue for people when the biggest storms you can imagine hitting anyone occur. Hell is proof of God's love and respect for all of us, for our independent nature. God will not make us do anything. Please do not think of hell as merely God punishing us for not getting enough good points to get into heaven. Hell is not so much punishment, as it is God giving us what we want. He will not force us to love Him or follow Him. If we choose to go our own way and ignore Jesus, then He will let us have our way. We can live for eternity without Him.

Here on the earth, even with terrible storms, there is still good, much more good than you realize, as we discussed in talking about finding peace by thankfulness. You still probably have some people in your life who care about you. You probably have a roof over your head and food to eat. Compared to so many hurting people around the world, or compared to my elderly or handicapped patients, most of us have much more than others. The point here is that anything in your life that is good and that you could be thankful for is something that is good and that comes from God. Any good in your life now is better than you would get in hell. This is meant to increase your contentment now for all you do have, things that you were not entitled to in the first place. It is all a bonus!

I talked earlier about a spoiled child who was upset because she did not get the exact Christmas present she wanted and then threw a big temper tantrum. We are all like this spoiled child. God has blessed us with many great presents in this life and the next. Yet, we complain that it is not enough. We have been given the most wonderful present in the world: salvation, from ourselves, hell, and loneliness. This gift is even more amazing when we compare it to the fact that we *should* be suffering terribly. How on earth could we ever be upset with not getting more gifts, when we have been given an amazing gift, the best gift ever? None of our problems, no matter how bad they are compares to what good we have been given.

And speaking about presents, do you know what the word "grace" means? It is one of those churchy words that we hear, but we are just supposed to know what it means. It means an unearned gift. God has given us a wonderful gift that we did not deserve. He gave it out of love. It is like someone who gives you a Christmas gift just because he loves you and for no other reason. He does not want anything in return. He just wants to do something nice for you. That is grace. That is who God is. All He asks is to accept it when you realize it is given to you. We do not deserve to be with Him or to receive any of His goodness that is still present today, even though we may be in a storm currently. Please realize that anything good we get in this life is icing on the cake thanks to God's goodness, grace, and mercy.

As I said throughout this book, I cannot deny you the right to feel sorry for yourself, at least, a little. Life will always be hard and sometimes downright torturous. I am not trying to take away your sadness if you have been a victim of life. But the truth is still there. There is good in this life, and the next life will be unbelievably good. Believe it—and have hope.

Chapter Takeaways

1. We want our lives to be fair. When we are in storms, it feels unfair.
2. Our own sin changes what is truly fair.
3. What we truly deserve due to our sins is death. What we deserve is hell.
4. God, in His amazing grace, gives us so much more than we deserve. Even in the worst storms of this life, we have more than we deserve.
5. We will get to be in God's presence in heaven, with not one single storm in sight forever, despite our sins.

Chapter 13

Final Thoughts

Congratulations! If you have made it this far in the book, then you must be serious about fighting the mental battle of depression that comes with the storms of life. It is not easy. It will never be easy. But you can get to a place of peace, regardless of who caused your storm. Indeed, you are getting there.

We talked earlier about the dangers of following one's own emotions. Emotions can negatively sway your thoughts and make illogical thoughts seem logical. Even though it was a negative thought that first started the emotion, this negative emotion then floods your brain with negative thoughts. In bad storms, some of these thoughts may very well be realistic and understandable, though not helpful in dealing with your current situation.

Now, hopefully after reading all this, you have minimized the irrational negative voices in your head and strengthened the positive voices, being mindful that the Captain in your head is listening to all of the voices and logically deciding what is best for you. On this side of heaven, some of your negative thoughts will continue to haunt you and try to bring you down. There will continue to be a battle of the head versus the heart and a battle of the tempting Devil on one shoulder and the angel of truth on the other.

Take the time and effort to write down some of the positive thoughts somewhere where you can see them. Change your environment. If you surround yourself with negativity, your thoughts will move toward the negative. You might love listening to sad songs when you are sad. Misery loves company, and it can help you feel understood and not alone. However, listening to these songs can bring you down further. Negative friends, who are also depressed, can keep your focus only on all of the wrong in your life and not what is good. Find a good church and Bible study. Put supportive, positive people around you. Listen to positive, encouraging music.

Many of the ideas in this book are just good, helpful advice for anyone, no matter what your religious views. Ideas such as accepting what you cannot change, and being thankful for what you have, are good for us emotionally regardless. However, many of the ideas in this book are only achievable through faith in Jesus Christ. This is exemplified in my numerous patients who have weathered terrible storms. Of course, I do not believe that faith in Jesus is blind faith. I believe with all of my scientific, skeptical, and analytical brain, and my heart, that a belief in Jesus is the only way. All science and rational evidence point to Him if you want to look. Many people are against Jesus, no matter what and do not want to consider the evidence.

To have the most solid sense of peace and joy, regardless of a bad storm, you must choose to believe in Jesus, and Jesus only. It would be great if you could just see how dearly He loves you and has done everything possible to bring you true happiness (John 3:14). However, it is not enough to just believe and be saved if you want to be as content in this world as possible. You must trust in Him daily.

There are two big parts of the Christian faith: salvation and sanctification. Salvation is the simple act of deciding in your heart and mind that you believe Jesus is real and died for you, and you need Him to forgive you. Salvation will bring you the ultimate happiness: heaven. But sanctification will bring you more happiness today.

Sanctification is the ongoing process of growing closer in your relationship with Christ. It involves trusting in Him on a deeper level and acting more like Christ in your behavior and the emotions of your heart. Just as in a marriage, when you love someone and take the time to get to know him deeper, you love more and trust him more, as a result, you grow happier in the marriage. Unfortunately, many of us have asked Jesus to forgive us, and it may have been real and genuine at the time, but that is as far as it ever went. There was salvation, but not sanctification. We do not learn anything more or spend any time with Jesus Himself to get to know Him. As a result, our happiness suffers.

Keep in mind that Jesus wants us to be good and do the right thing. But He knows we will always be short-sighted and often selfish children. He certainly longs for us to be good;

however, more than that, He longs for us to trust Him and keep coming back to Him. He wants us to trust that He knows what is best for us. He wants our hearts, souls, and minds (Luke 10:27). As we trust Him more, the calmer, more loving, and more at peace we are. We see the big picture and all the blessings we have, especially compared to what we deserve.

Conversely, the less we trust Him, the more we think we know how to handle our problems on our own. We think we know best. But time and time again, have you not proven you cannot make the best decisions for yourself? Is He the God who knows all, and loves you dearly, or isn't He? Do you believe that? Do you believe? If you believe it, then you will want to seek Him and be close to Him, for His sake and your own.

Pride: The Root of All Sin
What is the root of all sin, the core of your problems, with God and finding happiness in your life? Pride. But by pride, I do not mean just simple arrogance or hubris, as when someone says, "Look how much better I am than everyone else." Yes, it often means that. However, do not make the big mistake of thinking because you are not arrogant like this that you are not prideful. You may be a quiet, unassuming person, and still, be very prideful.

Pride can also be a simple thought that you deserve better; you want and thus think you deserve. If we have the expectation that life *should* be better, we are being prideful. We build up the "I," the sense of self that we deserve more. In the last chapter, we focused on what we really deserve. I did this to emphasize how ego-centric we are and how much our attention is just on ourselves.

Pride can also be simply wanting to do things our way. We want to have control over our lives. Each decision we make is either based on what God wants us to do or what we want to do. Whenever we do something we know we should not, in other words, sin, we are actively choosing to do it ***our way*** instead of ***God's way***. We think we know better than God at that moment. We are just like Adam and Eve.

Do we think we are smarter, wiser, or better than God Almighty? Are we that arrogant, as to think we know better than the Great I AM? When we are lazy, we are prideful. When we do not love our families or put others first, we are prideful. When we are overly depressed, we are not trusting in God and are prideful. When we are overly anxious, we are not trusting God and are prideful. But—we only hurt ourselves.

God made us. He designed us out of love. Doesn't it make sense that He knows what is best for us? If we want to know how to fix a broken computer, we go to the original engineer who built it. Likewise, we must go to the original Creator to get our lives fixed.

It is a simple premise. Do we, the simple-minded, short-sighted, self-centered created beings, know what is best for us better than the all-knowing, all-loving Father-God who created us?

Final Thoughts

God's rant to Job (Job 38) was a beautiful, well-laid-out argument to this end. God had to school Job who was the Creator and who was the created. He had to teach who was capable of making everything in the universe, and who was not worthy to demand anything of God. In the end, Job got the point and humbled himself before God and learned how to cope with extreme, hard times.

The more we see things from His perspective and learn to trust God, the more our lives improve. Some storms may be resolved just because we are no longer messing up and causing them. But even for other storms in which we are innocent victims, God can give us the strength and perspective to get through them much easier. If we trust in God, if we truly remember He is God, then we will know He will make lemonade out of lemons and work things out for our good (Romans 8:28). This does not mean He caused the storm, but He can make something great come out of it.

What does Jesus need us to do to help us to get through our storms? Be obedient and trust Him. I know obedience sounds like an uptight parental word and is not related to mental health. However, obedience naturally stems from trust. If we trust God who knows better than us, why don't we do what He advises? We should *want* to obey when the One giving the orders knows everything much better than we do and greatly loves us.

"I have been crucified with Christ and I no longer live, but Christ lives in me. The life I now live in the body, I live by

faith in the Son of God, who loved me and gave himself for me" (Galatians 2:20 NIV).

Convicted, But Hopeful

I hope this book leaves you feeling hopeful and inspired, even if a little convicted. I hope you stayed with it, took a hard look at yourself, and realized you could trust in God more and let go of yourself more. Convicted does not mean condemned, not at all. It just means you realize the truth, the truth of God's love and desire for you to be with Him and follow Him.

I love feeling convicted, and I always have. One of my favorite songs as a teenager was Scott Wesley Brown's song, "Lord, Lord." I think this was the title. It was such a lesser song on the album that no one knows it. I cannot even find it online now. The words of the song said, "Why do you call me Lord, Lord, when you don't do the things I say?" The words pushed me to do better, to love God in a more real way. I am not sure exactly what was going through my consciousness at the time. Maybe I felt comforted by this convicting song because it put me in my proper place.

I talked earlier about how our proper place is at God's feet, worshiping Him. For any of us to be convicted. We must first humble ourselves. We must admit we are in the wrong before God; we chose to go our own way over His and messed up because of it. When we feel convicted, we are at His feet. We are giving Him the recognition and respect He deserves.

"When I am weak, then I am strong" (2 Corinthians 12:11).

Final Thoughts

That song asks why we call Him, "Lord." Lord means one who is in authority over us. We pray to "the Lord." We call Him "Lord Jesus." In Christian circles, this is a commonly used term. I would imagine that most of us use the word as intended most of the time. But honestly, we only want Jesus to be our Lord when it is convenient, when we are in trouble, and we need Him. We really do not submit ourselves to His Lordship. We want to call the shots. We want control. Yet, we cry out to God, sometimes in anger at Him when things go bad in our lives. The specific storm in our lives may not be directly our fault at all. However, all of our storms are caused one way or another by Jesus not being His people's true Lord.

If you want to fight depression and anxiety, if you want peace in the middle of life's storms, make Jesus your Lord.

Monte's Praise Playlist

1. Praise you in this Storm – Casting Crowns
2. Great I Am – Phillips Craig, and Dean
3. Even If – Mercy Me
4. Heart Cries Holy – Big Daddy Weave
5. Holy – Nicole Nordeman
6. Holy God – Brian Doerksen
7. How Great is Our God – Chris Tomlin
8. How Great Thou Art – Chris Rice
9. Indescribable – Chris Tomlin
10. Jesus Messiah – Chris Tomlin
11. My Savior My God – Andrew Shust
12. On My Knees – Jackie Velasquez
13. Open The Eyes of My Heart (Whole "Worship" Album) –
14. Michael W Smith
15. Overwhelmed – Big Daddy Weave
16. Revelation Song – Phillips, Craig, Dean
17. Your Great Name – Natalie Grant
18. What A Beautiful Name – Hillsong United
19. Even When It Hurts – Hillsong United

About the Author

Dr. Monte Miller ("Dr. Monte") is a Christian Psychologist, not an academic, but one who has real-life experience being in the thick of helping clients professionally for over 30 years, and as a Christian minister since he was in high school through Young Life.

He is excited about this debut work, praying God will use it to help many. He has many other books in the works already.

After first reading books on relationships when he was 15 (a bit of a geek. And still has these two books in his primary bookcase), Dr. Monte went on to get his Master's and Doctoral degrees in Psychology. He had a successful 25-year career with his own nursing home practice before switching to a successful general adult online practice.

Dr. Monte prides himself on how comfortable clients of all types, shapes, sizes, and species feel with him. He tries to be the best husband he can be and is a first-rate cat dad with scars to prove it.

www.ingramcontent.com/pod-product-compliance
Lightning Source LLC
Chambersburg PA
CBHW050908160426
43194CB00011B/2327